CIRCE'S LAMENT

Circe's Lament

Anthology of
Wild Women Poetry

Edited by
Bianca Lynne Spriggs
and
Katerina Stoykova-Klemer

Accents Publishing • Lexington, Kentucky • 2016

Printed in the United States of America

Accents Publishing
Editors: Bianca Lynne Spriggs and Katerina Stoykova-Klemer
Cover Photo: Nadezda Nikolova-Kratzer

Library of Congress Control Number: 2015958196
ISBN: 978-1-936628-41-4
First Edition

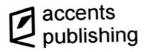

Accents Publishing is an independent press for brilliant voices. For a catalog of current and up-coming titles, please visit us on the Web at

www.accents-publishing.com

The editing and production of this anthology was made possible by a generous grant from the Kentucky Foundation for Women.

CONTENTS

II.

III.

This book is dedicated to the Kentucky Foundation for Women,
with gratitude for all they do.

In Greek mythology, Circe was considered an enchantress—she used potions and a wand to transfigure men into docile predators when they trespassed on her island. In *The Odyssey*, Circe most famously transformed members of Odysseus's crew into pigs when they gorged themselves on a feast in her mansion. As a consequence of abusing her power—specifically taking the life of her husband—some say that Circe was originally sentenced by her father, Helios, the sun god, to live out her immortal years in exile, unable to leave the island.

Circe's tale continues to resonate with us because even today, women continue to deal with the physical, emotional, and psychological ramifications of rejecting patriarchal values. Consequently, women characters are often exiled even in contemporary narratives: a woman makes the decision to leave her man; the woman is then punished by the patriarchy; the woman, bitter and jaded, takes epic revenge on all men unless she eventually finds herself wrapped up in another man. It's a sad state of affairs, the cautionary fable that continues to nest just beneath the surface of so many cultures around the world, continuing to dictate how we raise our daughters, how women reared in this tradition continue to formulate expectations of their relationships not just with men, but also with other women.

And yet, audiences continue to read Circe's story, mystified by her boldness. When we encounter her she is living in exile, but she retains her power despite being an outcast. Whether religious text, classical epic, or family lore, narratives of so-called "wild women" like Circe—amazons, monstrous mothers, destructive daughters, roots workers, weird sisters, goddesses, priestesses, warrior women, cyborgs, mermaids and other shape-shifters—have always fascinated us. We still wonder and speculate about legendary women: Cleopatra, Mary Magdalene, Kali, Mami Wata, Ishtar, Harriet Tubman, Annie Oakley. We wonder about our family members, our friends, the loves of our lives and the choices they made— what compelled them to act? What set them apart?

Women who break stereotypes and societal expectations continue to thrill our imaginations with how they did it. How did these women manage to balance their gender, sexuality, and power? Where did they find the strength to shoulder the consequences of rejecting the expectation of how women should behave? What do we continue to learn from the stories we tell one another of these icons, characters, and legends? What does a woman sacrifice in order to come into her own power? What does she mourn? What does she celebrate? This anthology seeks to answer these questions by highlighting the legendary, the local, the familial, and the self. It also explores the bigger question: Why do audiences continue over the ages to be spellbound by women who challenge and complicate convention?

Circe's Lament should certainly not be read as comprehensive in terms of the narratives we chose to highlight, but rather treated as a summoning, as a kind of welcome table. We hope that as you read through this host of poetry about wild women—from the classic to the contemporary, from the legendary to the little-known—you'll get the sense from their collective narrative that no woman ever needs to feel alone or exiled. It is our hope that you will read and celebrate, not just those highlighted in this collection, but all of the bold, bright, wild women in your own life.

—THE EDITORS

I.

ELLEN BASS

HOW I BECAME MISS AMERICA

There she is, Bert Parks is singing
and I am weeping as her gleaming teeth shine
through the wide-open window of her mouth.
When I grow up, I could be her.
Though I can't dance or sing
and girls fool enough to do dramatic
readings never win. But I've got time
and tonight my tears are hers,
falling like sequins down those lovely cheekbones.
I've just embraced the first runner-up,
who pretends to be happy for me,
sheaves of roses cradled, mink-trimmed cape
waltzed over my shoulders.
I'm starting down the runway.
My mother sips her highball.
My father leans back on the grease spot
his wavy hair has rubbed into the sofa.
We're six miles inland from Atlantic City
in a railroad apartment over Hy-Grade Wines and Liquors.
They worked all week selling Seagram's and cheap wine
and this is Saturday night. Summer. The windows raised
to catch whatever breeze might enter.
No one could predict that twenty-five years later
I'd be chanting *No more profits off women's bodies*
at the Myth California counterpageant
where Nikki Craft poured the blood of raped women
on the civic center steps, splashing
her ceramic replicas of Barbies:
Miss Used, Miss Directed, and *Miss Informed.*
And Ann Simonton, former *Vogue* model, posed as *Miss Steak*
in a gown sewn from thirty pounds of scalloped bologna

with a hot dog neckline and parsley garnish.
I'd just left my husband and come out as a lesbian.
My lover, in a tie and fedora, marched
with her poster, *Nestlé Kills Babies*.
That night we didn't need a moon.
From the minute my child fell asleep until we collapsed,
exhausted on her water bed, we made love
as one of Nikki's statuettes
in a glow-in-the-dark blue gown and tiara
watched over us, *Miss Ogyny*
painted in gold across her sash.

ROSEMERRY WAHTOLA TROMMER

WILD ROSE MAKES HER PLANE

What do you mean I am one minute late,
she says to the man in the suit behind the desk.
The plane is here. I am here. Here is my bag.
Put it on the plane.
The man behind the desk explains
that this would be impossible.
He does not look her in the eye.
Wild Rose smiles. *Everything is possible,*
she says.
She jumps across the baggage scale
and pushes the man out of the way.
Ma'am, he says, *I will get the police.*
Wild Rose says, *That's okay.*
She finds her name and gives herself
a first-class upgrade, prints out her tickets,
leaves her luggage for lost and walks
toward her gate. The man in the suit
stands there, phone still in hand.
He looks like a lost little boy. *Take me with you,*
he says to the space where she was.
She yells back, *You're one minute too late.*

PAMELA MILLER

TEN FACTS ABOUT THE AUTHOR
THAT MAY OR MAY NOT BE TRUE

for Nick Demske

1. On her opulent honeymoon in Bangkok,
   she repeatedly turned into a starfruit.

2. She has teeth inside her teeth inside her teeth.

3. Her code name is Good Golly Miss Anathema.

4. She is a tourmaline necklace.

5. Her poems are critiqued by flamingos.

6. She is allergic to anything.

7. She once attacked her mother with a headcheese.

8. She once stood shimmering in the Sistine Chapel,
   naked as a golden egg.

9. She dreams of a man whose spectacular fingers
   will open her like a jewel box.

10. On the last night of her life, she'll be swept away
    by a tsunami of her own ingenious making.

LUCIA CHERCIU

BLOSSOMING

She was not ugly; she was not beautiful.
Skinny, with a scarf that covered her face
when she rushed at night slinking by a fence.

When she smiled, her left cheek revealed
a birthmark, or maybe hid it. The men
who lived up on the hill knew her.

Her neighbors watched her gate,
the stealthy steps of summer, and counted
months for each of her three children.

The last one, blonde, with curly hair,
looked nothing like her mother
or her siblings. Whom she looked like

was her Godfather, who had held
the candles at her wedding, the valley
blossoming with gossip and gossamer.

DANNY

for Judith Anderson

I was beyond working
class poor. I was
the Italian kid

in a German town. I was
a baby bull dyke
Big Daddy, and the films

cooled my Midwestern
summers without air.
While my sister swam,

I submerged
myself in Hitchcock.
My dancer

of a mother insisted
I would love *Rebecca*.
The obsessed

maid character,
Mrs. Danvers, Danny,
moved so little

except for her eyes.
Buttoned up,
she floated through

the eaves of
my brain like a wraith.
Promised always to

wear black and frock,
to be forty-three
years old and crashing

with the burning frame
of the house loved
like a woman.

LEONA SEVICK

CUT AWAY
(after B.H. Fairchild)

I am not so young that I cannot see
what is happening here. Over sounds
of the dishwasher I hear voices.
My mother, asking the question over
and over again without heat or any real need
to hear him, sitting at the kitchen counter
with her book open maybe reading,
maybe not. My father, his head held low,
then lower still, circling behind her.
I hear her say more quietly
than I've ever heard her speak
Just tell me, just tell me now.
And he says *I have something to tell you.*

We watch an episode of M*A*S*H that I've seen
a dozen times, the one where Hawkeye
really loses it for good. He remembers
the Korean woman strangling a chicken on the bus
to keep it quiet. Sidney Friedman is called in
to dig deep, to uncover not a chicken but a baby.

My mother rushes from the bedroom where
she gathers me and my sister. She helps us
find our shoes, pushes us out the door, goes
back into the house to collect the guns.

Holding them carefully by the grips,
pointing them down like her father taught her,
she hands them over. I notice she has no shoes
on her feet, the red polish on her big toe is chipped.

JOAN JOBE SMITH

OUT OF SIGHT

To teach my out-of-sight hippie huz a thing or 2
for staying away 2 days and nights at a Love-In, I
took all his hippie clothes: his purple tie-dyed bellbottoms, his ratty rabbit fur vest, orange-magenta
madras cloth meditation p.j.'s, marijuana-leaf print
tank top and Jim Morrison black leather pants and I
played tug of war with our dog, a Doberman pinscher
whose sharp killer-shark teeth ripped them to shreds
the way we thought she'd do some day to a cat burglar
while I cooed: "Atta girl, atta girl, good dog, good dog."
Then I got all my hippie huz's beloved hippie albums:
LP's of the Beatles, The White Album, Rubber Soul,
3-Dog Night, Vanilla Fudge, Donovan, Rolling Stones,
Bob Dylan, The Doors, The Animals, Big Brother and
the Holding Company, Cream, Credence Clearwater,
Led Zeppelin, Steppenwolf, Canned Heat, Jefferson
Airplane, Country Joe and the Fish and I placed all
those licorice pizzas step-stones on the stairs leading
up to our bedroom while my good dog watched from
below until I called: "Here, girl, come to Mommy—"
and up, up she came, slipping, sliding but sure-foot
happy dog scratching zebra-stripes all over all those
hippie albums. "Good girl," I praised, "Out of sight!"
Later that night when hippie huz finally came home
sunburned, red-eyed from doing his own thing and
letting it all hang out at love-ins and saw the mess,
"MY GOD!" he exclaimed and asked. "WHAT THE
HELL HAPPENED?" and I answered: **I** didn't do it.

JOAN JOBE SMITH

THE GONAD STORY

At 15, anxious for my first diamond engagement
ring, I said Yes, I'd marry Jackie Lewis who'd just
quit high school to join the Coast Guard. I figured
when Jackie came home for Christmas with the
diamond ring, I'd wear it a few days to show off
to my girlfriends and then tell Jackie a Good Story
why I couldn't marry him. But the night before he
left for boot camp, I fixed him dinner (my parents
working late) and right after eating, Jackie lay down
on his stomach on my father's sofa in the den, placed
his hands between his legs and moaned: "Ohh—my
gonads. Ohh—my blue balls. Help me, help me,"
he moaned, reaching for my hand to help massage
the pain away that throbbed between his legs.
But I was only 15, had only been kissed two times
and didn't know about gonads even when he called
them testicles and begged me: "Help me, help me ..."
So I ran to the telephone to call an ambulance. "No,
no," Jackie moaned. "Only YOU can help me—" So
I ran to the bathroom for aspirin, to the kitchen for
a glass of water to splash in poor Jackie's face. So
Jackie got up and limped home and come Christmas,
he neither phoned nor gave me a diamond engagement
ring. He went back to his old girlfriend Gloria who had
big boobs and I'd become engaged four more times, been
married twice, a go-go girl for five years when I finally
figured out the plot of Jackie Lewis's convoluted, con-
trived Gonad Story—a story as old as the trilobites who
first whispered it, same story later painted in Cro-Magnon
caves—that lecherous little male chauvinist pig plagiarist.

ELSA VALMIDIANO

NABOKOV IN THE BATHROOM

Nabokov would retreat to the bathroom to write.
He shared a one-bedroom with his son and wife.
Where else was he supposed to write?
I had tried the same thing once.

In my burgundy lingerie and furry slippers,
I had retreated to the bathroom to write
in the middle of the night.
I usually have a fear of bathrooms
in the middle of the night.
The cold tiles. The mirror in the dark
reflecting nothing but my childhood imagination
of a frightening lady with blood, scars, and
dark eyes waiting on the other side.

I had a lover then.

On some nights when it was too late or
we were too lazy to insist upon him going home,
he slept in my bed, or rather jostled, in my tiny studio.
Only when he was over, my mind
would crash and roar and tumble
with what I believed were poems,
when they were merely false alarms
for beautiful explosions.

I would wait till he had fallen asleep,
his legs kicking madly across the bed,
and I would slip away and bring a tea light
in a square-shaped glass
into the bathroom with me,
and I would sit on the toilet, laptop on lap,

invoking Nabokov, when I realized I had no patience
or business writing on the toilet as I did, for as I did,
my lover would wake up like a little child afraid of the dark,
calling me from bed,
and wondering
why I was taking so long in the bathroom.

I was writing, trying to write,
with a candle flickering in the darkness.
I sat, frustrated, interrupted.
In that failed attempt
I still feel the smoothness of that burgundy lingerie
falling above my knees
and the lace above my breasts
sliding against my skin as I shifted uncomfortably on the toilet,
my bare feet slipping out of my furry slippers onto the cold tiles,
with the tea light flickering in the square-shaped glass.
I thought of Nabokov then. Only Nabokov.

SHERYL NELMS

THE PHARMACIST'S DAUGHTER

It was August first 1955

I knocked on their leaded glass door
collecting on my paper route
for the Sweetwater Register

old man Dimmers owned the drugstore
and they had a real
nice two-story house

I started to knock
again

when I saw Mary Alice
prancing down
those spiral
stairs

one step
at a
time

sixteen and so blonde
in her black bra
and panties

all of her was jiggling

I was ten years old
and I never
ever

saw anything
like that
before

she swung that door open

"Hey, Russell," she said
"Come on in and I'll
find your money"

but I left
didn't say nothing

never could catch my breath

TINA PARKER

STOP

No we're not playing baby any more
Get up
You can walk
Use big girl words

Sit down or you're not getting dessert
You have a napkin right there
Why are you wiping your mouth with your sleeve

Why are you doing that
Please let me eat
I need my arm
You're hanging on it

Stop kicking her
You're not going to bite your sister
We don't hit

I don't know why I plan things for you to do
With your friends when you act like this
If you want to hear the song stop talking
Leave her alone

Just close your mouth and be quiet
I'll tell you when to come out
I'm not ready to see you

We're going to turn that off in a minute
You have five more minutes
No there are no more minutes it's time to go
Come on I'm leaving

Just a minute
Get your hands off me
I don't like the hitting hands
Use your words

No I can't
You know how to put them on yourself
It makes my back hurt
Because I'm mean

Tina Parker

THE DAY MY FOUR-YEAR-OLD SCRATCHED ME

I scratched her back
It broke the skin
I knew I'd be turned in

I prayed it would heal
By the time she went to school

In the tub that night she cried
Oh my boo boo hurts
How did I get this boo boo mama

She said maybe from my hair thing
When it was on my wrist

And I did not correct her.

ELLEN HAGAN

PICTURE THIS

for Miriam Dawson Hagan, or Mamaw & her wildest woman self

If it's the last pink salad syrupy-sweet that you'll eat
cooled whip, coconut & walnuts & the last stuffing sliced
w/ onions in their thin skins—sage & salt. If it's the last
& it is—cornmeal fried to bread—go ahead & relish.

Remind your gullet to savor New Haven's winding roads
& the goats in yards & the blind folded wheelbarrow game
Papaw calling porch rules & seven aunts & uncles & 16 cousins
w/ all their legs & bodies stained w/ grass, their raucous laughs.

See Miriam Dawson Hagan as she was—not at the end—littered
breath, uterus falling—all the children weighing her smallest
body down, down. & the one they lost—ninth—& Uncle Joe
whose bulbous lungs became ocean & his body floated away.

Years chiseling skin to dust, her humped spine—curved, curling.
Don't see the fade, or the slow motion. See her still weekly hair-do
bouncing w/ its curl & the corsage of carnations at her breastbone. See
her ripe, wily, pouring grease into skillets, frying, her lap, apron slung.

See her down the river—bathing suit, cap & your own fish of a mother—
warning you of snakes, the deep end, all the fish & fins & teeth, warning
you of New Haven & its country & its hillbilly ways &
who swims in rivers after all?

Now see your Mamaw as she was—swimming—smile like a dare,
w/ her bare, young legs, toes flirting with crawdads—watch her sly,
study her quick—tendons, muscles all in.

CAROL QUINN

SOLILOQUIES AT THE OUTER BANKS

CRO

—inscription found at the site
of the abandoned colony of Roanoke

1. Lost Painting by John White

Following their feasts and practices, a daughter
of the Picts keeps watch at arms before
the thatch and windmills of our present future.
The stippled flowers of her skin are bare.
Engravers' copies of the painting hint
at what the Roman garrisons saw more
than my soft sketches and unpiercing paint.
A father's gentleness? Adventurer
and expedition artist, I came to lead.
My daughter was among the settlers
at Roanoke. If I idealized
the land, the crops still failed. They found no pearls.
Yet she believed—as if in trees sketched with
the very charcoal left when they'd been razed.

2. Lost Colony

Outside, leaves stick. Ragged newsprint clings.
That which preserves, contains—one changed reminds
me: they have flickering, unbroken wings.
They feel their way like human hands.
Now turquoise, teal, indigo in motion—
sometimes they black out deep in their oblique,
then come back like the first light on the ocean.
But underneath, they're rain-soaked bark.
Through masks of branches, eyespots blink and glance

away. Mid-sentence, satellites go dark.
You seemed to see. *Windows* once meant *eyes
of wind.* The wings' reflective markings are
like windows in a blighted city: blind,
walled-in eyes of wind. *No longer look for me—*

3. Croatoan

I waited for a sail to return.

I waited while the cannons rose and gold
was lifted from a dayless depth to shine.

Let this story's ending go untold.

On different shores, we will become
the other's myth: the pearl that forms around
the grain that we remember, a word that named
the meeting place—or syllable that sounded
like a bird that carries fire.
                                    The smoke of sand
fills in your tracks (but you gave up the search
too soon). I want to turn back from the sea.
In braids the quartz unravels. Shells will be
chaff shoals, and all will churn and break and wear
to whispering dunes of bitter, blowing sand.

4. Lost Letter

This coast subdues. The currents bank the shards
of what is cast, outcast, endlessly tossed—
and sand collects and passes through like words.

Though you will never hear, I still resist
and write as water fills the hull: a letter
to be found among the amphoras and rust.

We knew our galleon was lost and let
its freight of ponies go. It would be cruel
to make them share in our ship's fate.

Let me go, my love, and grow forgetful.
Unmoor the anchor; cut the ghost cord
that connects us in the dark (if not the light).

The sand reminds me of you. I do not fear
its pale of wrists and lips, its whispered prayer.

5. Assateague

Letting go, the fallen waves pull back
across the gasping surface of the sand.

They leave what they have filched from rock
and wrecks. The low pines fitted to the wind

hold fast as they at last release their sand.
I lose my way. The present has no maps.

How quickly roads and houses are abandoned.
The wind performs its ongoing eclipse.

New forms appear. A head emerges from
the body of the sea. Soon there will be

a band of them reliving their escapes
and passages, their uncut manes half foam

until they stand like newborn foals, shake free,
and gallop from the present's gray collapse.

JESSICA WRIGHT

SUMMER IN REHAB, AND WHAT DO YOU TELL ME? YOU MET THIS GIRL, WHO MIGHT HAVE BEEN A BIRD

If she was a bird, she'd be a wren:
a light stepper, eyes fine as threads,
hair like sun on the bare arms
of a beech tree in winter.

She wore herself like a dress
she had inherited: stiff velvet
streaked silver with dust, pulled taut
over its slender-knuckled frame.

She knitted like the Fates,
dipping her needle into the pool of her yarn.
From her fingers flew foxes
and dragons, blackbirds, bats, a unicorn;

one morning, six snails paraded
across her breakfast table,
shells out of brown paper
antennae in knots.

Quiet in the dining room,
she carved her toast into nets
and studied her peas as if each
viridescent sphere was a planet,

in which she might tell
all our fortunes.

THE GIRL AND THE END OF THE WORLD

She has no interest in guns. Crossbows, yes. Tasers—maybe. But the cold hard fact of a gun in the house makes her remember the guns from years before. The racks. The little hidden silver pieces in drawers of folded boxers. The live wire always a threat.

Water is most important. You have to have water. Stockpiles of water. Extra cases. Water cleaning tablets. Water filter straws. The polar bears are eating dolphins. Water's on sale through Wednesday—BUY 2 FOR $4. She is running out of time. Time will end. The sky will break. The hum of refrigerators and TVs will go silent. The people will all walk out of their homes and stand in an orange light, holding hands. Whispering what's next. Don't tell them you have extra food. Don't tell them you have painkillers. Don't tell them you have cigarettes. They will turn into monsters. Extensions of the Devil's toes. Their faces will wrinkle with terror and their fingernails will scratch at the ground. Hunger must be conquered. She's practiced for months. Not too bad. You just get dizzy. And your muscles don't work. More sharpies. She needs to finish the expiration dates on the powdered milk baggies, the spam, the ramen noodles and the breakfast bars. 2020, 2019. All so different, how will she keep track? It's the perfect balanced meal plan for maximum protein and minimum weight. She will have to carry this bin with her to the closet— the basement—the bathroom. Crank radio that charges cell phones. Cell phones that read email. Text alerts. Go up to the sky and come back down. Unleashed. Tiny little computers that hold the authority on time. Until time stops. *We will burn the organ for heat. The guitars and the piano. We will sharpen the records into daggers. Strap kitchen knives to our waists. Put on a pair of sturdy shoes. Stay calm and look to the cross. It's all over the place with these people. Do they think God will save them? God is going to destroy them. And you just need a few gallons of water. What's wrong with you? Where's your bug-out bag? Your extra cat food? Your bloodstop that works on horses and humans too? Will you bleed until you can bleed out? Come into my garden and rape the fruits of my labor? It's too late to save the heirloom seeds. It's too late to get that summer deal on metallic blankets that will keep you warm.* This Christmas, she will divvy up the best of her tools—the auto gas shutoff crank, the weather radios, the flashlights and matches, the stun-guns, the hatchets, the saws. The nieces will get water straws in pink. The mothers will get radios they can clip to their pants. The fathers will get first-aid kits and emergency lights and pocketknives. They will be ready. They will stay safe. The masks are hard to fit. They're too bulky. They won't stack right in the bin. Should she have gotten more than two? *Remember to put the mask on yourself first before assisting others.* Will she really be able to breathe or will she panic like she did when she tried to go snorkeling? Well, guess that's why there's duct tape. Shelter in place—in what place? The bedroom? Which window has fewest cracks? Which wall is thickest? Which room where we curl up and die? She is behind. Nothing goes together. She has too many band-aids and not enough cutting things. Add cutting things to the list. Search for sale on Amazon–and Prime it so it gets here in two days. Is it illegal to have this stun gun? Cracks like lightning. Straight to the neck. Or into the thigh. *Will it be a neighbor? Or will it be a stranger rampaging through, smelling fires and food? Will it put them down? Will it stop them from coming? Hide the bin. Quick.* She throws the rest inside and closes the lid. Waterproof tight. Yanks the vacuum from the pantry and slides the bin in. Covers it with extra paper towels, toilet paper and ziploc boxes. Slams the door tight. They cannot know how prepared she is. They cannot know she has food for months. They cannot know she will fight them to survive. They cannot know she will not win. She is too weak to lift her End-of-World bin. Arms too flaccid. Her gait is wrong. She will not run. And cannot breathe. Without her medication, her asthma will kill her. Without her medication, she will drown in her own lungs. Without her medication she will wail and shake and crumble to the floor, bruising her knees. She writes: *I built this kit for you. I gave you water and warmth so that you can survive. I gave you tools so that when you are born, you can fight. I found the perfect balance of protein so that you can grow strong. I added candy so that you could taste joy. I sealed up the back-up phone charger so that you could have a lifeline. And I gave you light so that you could travel across the city to escape. A hatchet so that you could cut yourself out. I gave you a name. You would have made me mother. But you stopped short. You missed the boat. You got tangled up. And you told me so. Your small and strange world ended on a table in the hospital we didn't know. This big and strange world continues on, like a nightmare. We are screaming but nothing comes out.*

JULIA JOHNSON

THE WOMAN IN THE CITY

She waited, driftwood body stung by wasp,
her folded hand like a knife. She was irritable, too
lifeless to wait any longer. The radio rattled and she
remembered her stroke in the stream. She turned like a top,
in, and then once out, she was bright as golden hair. The
trees bristled in the open air. She looked back, the orange
of her dress like an unpredictable peach. Her thumbs held to
her shoulders; it was twelve o'clock. She worried about
something other than her hands. They had helped her,
she knew, in the brassiest and smallest way. The breeze died
down around her smooth head.

FRANK X WALKER

YOU HIT LIKE A GIRL

for Brenda,

You always preferred the rough and tumble
over Easy-Bake, Barbie dolls, lace.
When you planned a tea party after school
everybody came to watch you be as ugly as Joe Frazier.

If our small Kentucky town hadn't been so traditional
you would have earned your Golden Gloves
in the ring, with other light heavyweights
instead of doing time in the principal's office

You raised frogs in my biceps with your sharp knuckles,
stole punches to my chest, dared me to cry.
You married a stubborn fool,
a legal excuse to fight in the streets every night.

When I hold you, palms up, through two inches of glass,
your baggy orange jumpsuit framed by institutional gray,
you flinch at my eyes that measure you like fists,
then swing at you in slow motion down my cheeks.

When I deliver the news, your knees buckle.
I lower my hands, stare down at you convulsing
on the floor. The chaplain hovers like a cut man.
All of us wait   for the bell.

FRANK X WALKER

TIME IS THINNER THAN GLASS

I had forgotten you were my first kiss
until I see you standing there
behind my sister, waiting quietly.

Your half smile tells me you remember
too, so I pretend to ignore
the orange jumpsuit swallowing your curves.

In that chasm between my lips
and her ear, I search for words
I haven't found strength to rehearse.

Hand dancing through two inches of glass,
I manage a "mama's gone" and watch her
legs quit—her heaviness fold like paper

into your ready arms. The receiver swings
like a dead man. Time bends. I close my eyes
and kiss you, again. This time it's for real.

LUCILLE LANG DAY

DELINQUENT SONNETS

1. In Juvenile Hall

New Juvie has bright paintings on the walls
to celebrate the better things in life:
nature, growth, transformation. These murals
admonish, "Graduate! Put down your knife."
Mustard-colored cells are stacked in tiers,
windowless, with built-in cots and stools,
where teenagers, alone, confront their fears
and contemplate new ways to break the rules.

The year I was thirteen I ran away
from home and landed here. Back then my cell
had a window. I could watch grass sway
on a hillside, hear jays and warblers call.
More pleasing than a work of art to me:
a glimpse of sky, a hummingbird, a bee.

2. Wild Kid

I finally have become the proper girl
my mother always wanted me to be.
I don't smoke hash or grass, wear mini-skirts,
pick up long-haired, tattooed men or party
till the neighbors call the police. My last
drunken binge was nineteen seventy.
My motorcycle-riding days are past.
I haven't shoplifted since sixty-three.

Oh, Mama, what's to become of me?
I've no regrets for anything I did—
the mescaline, the baby at fifteen.

Inside, I'll always be your wild kid.
I'd gladly wear those mini-skirts again
if I had the legs I did back then.

LINDA CASEBEER

THE GIRL

She has no money she has no wallet
her photo ID stolen she says
she has no driver's license
she has no proof of a marriage license
or the official divorce decree
since her ex husband had a job
she has no Medicaid
she has no food stamps
she has no food
she has no place to live
she has no rent money
she has a social security card
she has a birth certificate
she has an iPhone5 a gift
she has clean drug tests
she has an infant Faith Ann
she has visitation twice a week for an hour
she has to bring her own supplies
but the bag is empty
she has no money for supplies
she has a toothache
but she has no dentist
she has no birth control
she says she could never kill a baby
but her mother once told a judge
she would kill her three stairstep
children before she would let them
live with their father the fourth
child she gave up for adoption
the girl has a diagnosis of depression
she has samples of an antidepressant

but she has no prescription to refill
she has a history as a ward of the state
and a runaway
to get money from disability
that claims she cannot get a job
because she is borderline psychotic
the snow is half a foot deep
she has no boots she has no gloves
she has no scarf
she has a hand-me-down denim
jacket with a broken snap at the top
from a grandfather who says
she is a piece of shit mother
words that run through her veins
but she has a good heart
she says when she turned eighteen
there were ten different men
on Facebook who invited her to move in
she has an account on Meet Me
where she met her current man
who lives with his parents
she has moved in with them
she has a message on her Facebook
wall written by her ex husband
that says *whore* she has more exes
than she can count
she has a new baby scrapbook
to record memories for her child
she has one trash bag
she has a 12 x 12 inch cardboard
box for her possessions

she has a fairy tale
her mother told her that a true love
will carry her away and take care of her
and live with her happily ever after
world without end Amen

TERESA MILBRODT

LAURA

In the grocery store line with white bread, bologna,
yellow mustard lunch, Marlboros for dessert.
I loved how you knew to prioritize, buying a meal
for everyone in the office, sharing cigarettes with Earl

and talking in your Brillo pad voice—*Little Girl,*
You're giving me stress—then spending the afternoon
on computer solitaire and chatting with cousins
when they wandered in with grandbabies. Laura

standing in the gravel parking lot after work,
hills stretched before us rolling out the entire state
of South Dakota, and you with another cigarette—
did you ever keep count?—saying, *Stay here with me,*

Little Girl, until my daughter gets here. Your hair
like a helmet, didn't move despite never-ceasing breeze
on the plains. That was you, a warrior, though you
never told me of your battles, just hinted, with sly

comments about the first and second ex-husband. Laura
with fingers I was sure could dent a tin can. Laura
whose every fourth word was an expletive. Laura
who punctuated laughs with fits of coughing. Laura,

You should have been a goddess of something, tenacity
or bulldozers or red hot cinnamon candies, since your
every Friday night plan was to go to Casino and pick up
young men. You said, *They like older women 'cause*

we know what we want. You shook a cigarette from the pack,
fumbling for your lighter and one more shot of fire.

BARBARA CROOKER

JANIS

She sang to all of us who never fit
in, too bony, too fat, too weird, wired
all wrong for the cliques of a Texas high
school, the religion of football, cheerleaders,
jocks, longnecks, pickup trucks, madras A-lines,
bubble cuts, penny loafers.
What's amazing is she stayed as long as she did—

Take another little piece of my heart, now, baby—
When she sang, she put the pedal to the floor,
hundred miles an hour and a brick wall straight ahead.
And there was *nothing* straight about this girl,
hot pink feathers flying out of her hair, silver
bracelets up to her elbows, chunky rings on every finger,
their own kind of ball and chain. Granny glasses,
glassy-eyed full-stoned grin. Voice like a rasp,
a jar full of nails, shaking.

If, in the end, it all went wrong, well, Janis,
you never just showed up, you always gave it
everything you had. *Look down on us,* now,
the acne-scarred, the greasy-haired, the unbeautiful.
Stomp your leg like a piston building up steam,
thrust and jut your skinny hips, shimmy and shine.
Sing *Summertime* as one loud moan of pain
through the gravel and broken glass in your throat.
You know you got it if it makes you feel good.

LUCILLE LANG DAY

ANGENETTE SAMPSON
Dartmouth, Massachusetts, 1880

Thirty years old, live-in housekeeper,
she'd never wed or loved a man
and didn't think she ever would,
but that spring the Indian came
to plant parsnips, leeks and corn,
feed chickens, and milk the cows
on the Hazards' farm for a fraction
of a white man's wage. Her breath
quickened each day when he arrived.
She noticed his muscles, cheekbones,
long black braids, and he accepted
the coffee she brought to the barn.

The Wampanoags lived in shacks
by the pond outside of town.
She'd never been there but knew
the Indians were nearby and poor.
He brought her flowers, stones
and shells, said he was the *sachem,*
his people's leader. He loved her,
he said, but they couldn't go away.
She gave birth to a daughter
the following year, wouldn't tell
the father's name. The Hazards
fired him, but said she could stay.

SOLACE

When Master realized I was the only white girl still bleeding with the moon, the others too sick with Ireland, forbidden, in their blood, he ordered me to the breeding hut. And I was fed, green beans, red apples, and given another dress made out of sugar sacks and twice a day a black man was unchained outside the hut, forced through the door. The drivers leaned, watching. I made sure I was kneeled over the cot, coarse dress round my waist, before they came in. I didn't want to see their eyes shining with hate at my pale face. Even the women, who used to whisper in Irish, forbidden, through the cracked planks at feeding time, hate me, my burn fading, my cheekbones less like shelves for hungry eyes. And it went like this for months, at least three times I bled alone. And then Not John was brought to my door. And they had to whip him before he'd cross over the threshold. And when he came to me, my face already pressed against the rough canvas, my eyes, thighs already braced against his entrance, he growled, pulled me to the dirt floor by my red hair. His cane-cutting hands, rough with work, shredded my sack dress, made painful stripes on my breasts, and when I whimpered, he shook me. The driver laughed. And when I was in his shadow, when he pushed into me, I looked at his face. And his shimmering molasses-hate eyes didn't see me, just white. And he used his body against that white. And I wanted him to see I was Irish, forbidden. I wrapped my limbs around his cross-scarred trunk, held as hard as I could. I whispered some scraps of an old Irish, forbidden, lullaby, the only offering I had to make. He wept inside me. He yelled something ancient and rage-filled, forbidden. The planks rattled, the air stood thick. The drivers stopped laughing. He dried his face with my hair. He left, crawling out into hot Barbados sun. I curled up, a child in the dirt, and cried, cried Ireland, forbidden, cried sweet cane juice. No driver brought him back that afternoon.

MEG EDEN

PERCEPTIONS OF FREEDOM

Last month Micki bought a taxi. Said she was tired
of doing papers and wanted to make something new
in her life. After lunch, she showed it to me:
a used minivan with the word TAXI emblazoned
on the side. In that parking lot, we were both
dreamers still—I imagined her picking me up
from school, the profits saved up for our trip
to Ukraine. Next time I saw her though, she was
back in her jeep, the windows filled with newspapers.
The taxi's gone, she said, *too complicated
to do business here. Regulations, bureaucracy—
this state's got it all.* We laughed and talked
about our slim pickings of good single men around here.

That night she drove me home, she said: *At least
I'm not at a desk.* And whenever I returned
to work the next day, I thought to myself,
At least I'm not in a car.

Susan Johnson

CAGE

Because Grandmother made
the best bread, mother refused
to learn, refused the flour,

the living culture she would not
keep alive, culture of women
trapped in a kitchen as if

in a hive. I worked there,
she told me, pointing to a Boston
storefront once buzzing

with books. The cashier sat
high above the stacks in a cage
that was no cage to her.

Patricia Wellingham-Jones

THE BIKER GIRL

wears long hair curled
in blonde-grey spirals
way down past her shoulder
blades tickling her hips
She flashes a scarlet smile
that lights up downtown
Eyes snap like a late-night
campfire
Leathers hug her thighs
and her biker vest is snug
as a starlet's T-shirt
She takes off into the sunset
with a blast
that blows birds off trees
Sends a postcard home
every week
to her granddaughter

MEG EDEN

THE TICKET FOR WIVES
AT THE ANNUAL WOODWORKING SHOW

The ticket my father hands me reads: $2 OFF ADMISSION FOR SPOUSE.

The woman at the counter asks: Is this your wife?

My life needs no police investigations. I am not a mail-order bride, not a Mormon daughter-wife. My father is thrifty and forgets my birth date. I am seventeen and have never been kissed.

But the woman does not ask for my testimony. She stamps our hands and lets us enter the woodworking show. We are in the middle of a fairground, and I realize, people do not ask questions, here.

The only women in the show are old, married to men with shirts that read: He Who Has the Most Tools Wins. These men do not look at me or talk to me. They ask my father what he likes to make, and he pats my back, says, My daughter is the real craftsman here. They always look surprised when I sit at the scroll saw and cut out plywood hearts—small and easy to break—I make them in one cut to display how quickly I can turn, how thin and smooth the outside edge is.

It is then that I am made known.

II.

JOANIE DIMARTINO

SHE SELLS SEASHELLS

"Sally Brown, She's a pretty little craft ...
Sharp to the fore, with a rounded aft ..." [†]

She's not their first salt.

Before her was the sea
in summer, where they dove naked
into waves as boys

will do, wrestle tide swells,
currents, and each other

until the years their energies
center in their loins:
        then they come to her,

with newly-lowered voices

and whisper how they prefer
the sea sweetened
with a woman's sweat ~

the moist oyster
between a woman's legs,
her hidden pearl
they pay to coat with a salty
nacre, the single
bed sheet perfumed

of mollusks licked
with high tide foam
at shoreline.

She often walks the beach
at sunrise, when the tired moon's
shimmer has gone adrift ~

dips her fingers
in the sea, tastes fresh salt,

     blesses her lips.

† "Sally Brown" was the generic name given by sailors in sea chanteys to represent the women on shore they pined for, especially women of easy virtue. The epigraph of this poem is taken from the chantey, "Fire Marengo."

SARAH FRELIGH

EASY

A cop caught me naked
from the waist up the night
I parked with a boy behind

a construction site, high beams
of my bare breasts white
as the bra wadded up

on the console, the dress
I sewed that afternoon
tossed over the front seat.

It looked so good I'd hated
to take it off even when he begged
me to, even as his fingers

marched up my spine, zipper's
whisk the same sound my
scissors made on first cut, crisp

and final. Hope is a dress
you assemble from three yards
of cotton, fashion a self

to step into. How easy
to give her away.

AMY WATKINS

VOICING DESIRE

Years later, and she's still silent in bed.
She's learned to say grace, but sings only alone.
Her shimmering scales are so easily shed:

silk and blue-green sequins slipping over her head
like waves, she thinks, though she hasn't been home
in a squid's age. She is silent in bed.

The prince is a fine lover, parts her red
hair with deft fingers, talks dirty, moans.
Her shimmering scales are a dress she sheds

only with lights off. His voice, disembodied:
Yeah, you like that. He wants her to groan
like a mammal, but she's always silent in bed.

She tries out phrases, revises in her head—
Make me feel like I'm drowning—words like fish bones—
Fuck me like the shimmering creature I shed.

She can't express what she wants or the deep dread
that the voice she got back wasn't her own.
After so many years, she's still silent in bed,
her shimmering scales, now a dress she can shed.

STAR COULBROOKE

SHOPPER

My platform sandals went to the grocery store
in the nineteen-seventies
at the bottom of white linen bellbottoms
tight at the butt and thighs, no panties.
I was nineteen, with two kids.
My legs were long and tan,
showed tan right through the weave,
darker at the crotch, a heart-shaped pussy.

You were there bagging groceries at sixteen,
you tell me now, thirty years later,
and though my toenails were lacquered
red in those sandals
and my feet were supple as tulips,
you wanted only what the pants covered.
But oh, if you only knew
that touching me between the toes
or in the arch and ball, unbuckling those sandals
and stroking me there
would bring me to orgasm every time,
what would you give to put that in a bag
and drive home with me?

CATHERINE PERKINS

RECIPE FOR TOE FLAMBÉ

Ingredients needed:

1 female body (14 years or older)

1 male body, over 18 and at least two years older than the female (males mature later than females)

a dash of beauty (either or both bodies)

2 cups of semi-long (about 10"–15") hair, any color

1 pint of cheap whiskey

Directions:

Put the male behind the wheel of a nondescript car,
rev it up with a whisk, add the teen female,
stir vigorously until well-blended. Make sure
the toes and hair are folded in. The hair is key
for binding purposes. Let stand while the oven preheats to 350 degrees.
Make sure the male and female remain well-blended.
He will try to separate and rise to the top.
Watch out for the toes! They know how to walk.
If you whisk too hard curdling will be an issue.
If the toes get into the male's mouth you might as well toss
the entire batter because the teenage girl
will be tired, spent and flat, unable to rise during the cooking process
and the male will be done before the oven is hot!
Bake for 30 minutes.
Remove from oven, pour whiskey over and set afire.

Teneice Durrant

ANOTHER WOMAN

After our work of shuffling
between tables and kitchen, fetching
and smiling and nodding, we go out
for drinks, sit in a barely-lit bar,
and you dare me to smoke
your cigarette, tease
me because, I confess, I've never
inhaled. I take the dare because
we are drunk, and your pale eyes, ringed
with mascara hold some mystery.
But instead of putting
the Marlboro to my lips, it is your own
pink mouth pushing wet smoke
past my tongue, your fingertips pressing
the back of my neck
so I can't pull away. My lungs catch
the cloud you give me
and I cough, hard, as if breathing
for the first time.

LAURA MADELINE WISEMAN

CANDY, CIGARETTES, AND FAIRIES

At the free special exhibit opening on contemporary
fairy folk art at the university art museum, I'm sure
fairies are hiding behind the trees in the photograph,
behind the girl, the one like your sister, with the candy
cigarette. This is America, the late 1980s of outlandish
white ruffles, plastic wristwatches, hair sun-bleached
and wild. We let summer turn our skin tawny. We
say we want boys because that's what the movie girls
say—heroes, stone mansions, big plastic boobs, shiny
SUVs. All of us have kid sisters, some brother climbing
the ladder, blurred in our background. We face the
flickering of *Do it!* because that's what girls do. This
landscape, fairies, girls, and ladder-brother, that is
meant to be us, meant to be America, is everything
I remember—fountain drinks, nickel candy from
the bottom shelf, bubble gum tattoos, fairy lip balm.
America, do you believe in fairies? America, put your
queer girl shoulder right here. Snap your fingers.
America, don't die.

BRITT ASHLEY

FILM ADAPTATION OF A LOVE SCENE
FROM MY UNREAD COPY OF WUTHERING HEIGHTS

We open with a wide-angle shot of perfect misanthropy, all pears and
desolation. I love your eyebrows, the way everything sounds French
for no good reason and most of all, your ridiculous name. The kind of
name given to a boy raised by lions after he is finally brought home,
shaggy, royal, and confused. *This is a cup, a knife, a kiss, a plateful of dinner
that never ran from you.* Still, you keep meat in inappropriate places,
secret rare steaks in the library, nestle tender legs of lamb in dresser
drawers. I tend wolves in the nursery and pretend not to notice. Before
you, I loved beyond my means, loved a girl so fiercely I swallowed my
tongue before I could tell her. So now I am all brindle and howl, spoiled
bitch, all yours.

TINA ANDRY

PERMANENT

I want a tattoo
of your name
on the place
that hurts
most

KATERINA STOYKOVA-KLEMER

ONE SHOULD EXERCISE CAUTION

when kissing a daffodil.
Somebody could get hurt.
It helps to have dabbled in botany.
To reach the Sweet of Hearts
without splitting apart her innermost
petals is a high art. While the kiss lasts,
you'll share her crown.
You'll shimmer in the sun for days
after you drift apart.

KISSING A KNIFE

is a whole different practice.
It requires cautious recklessness
and commitment
to your own suffering.
What matters most, of course,
is that you love
the knife—
both smooth and sharp.
You receive the beauty of your face
reflected in his sides
as a holy sacrament.
He combs your hair
with his serrated crown,
and I pity the fool who tries
to save your life.
From that point on,
your blood belongs
on the outside.

BIANCA BARGO

I DON'T KNOW WHY I SUCKED YOUR DICK

that Monday in your shitty apartment
with the window open to the warm sun
and the sound of Kroger shoppers
across the street.

It was the first time I tried to swallow
up someone I didn't love.

It may have been impulse, the sick pull
in my stomach when I stand at high windows
and feel the urge to fling myself through them.

It may have been to prove I could,
the way I would when I was just a girl—
I'd jump the creek banks pretending
I wasn't scared to wake the snakes
cooling themselves beneath the rocks.

It may have been for the same reason
I've plucked a penny from the pavement:
because it was there. And honestly
it was so delicious-thick, it reached for me
and I felt compelled to answer.

It may have been to forget myself
and the gifts I give in love and for love,
to say fuck love altogether and instead
to understand lust, own it, admit
I'm animal, driven by the gustatory.

It may have been to own *you,*
that part at least, to lap and
suck and pump it, yes,

but also to know
I could bite it off
if you crossed me.

It was probably just so I could write this poem.

MARIAHADESSA EKERE TALLIE

BRAZEN HUSSY BLUES

I like a man who's handy
makes my house feel good as new
he don't need no tool kit
when we hammer, nail, and screw

some gals are fine with one man
I've always needed two
cause what the first can't handle
the second sho can do

once I get my two men
I go find number three
morning noon and night
I got some sweet thing next to me

people say i'm brazen
I say *well that ain't news*
you at home washing dishes
wishin you was in my shoes

cryin over some man?
none can have my heart to bruise,
there ain't no such thing
as the brazen hussy blues

CACTUS CLUB DANCER, AFTERNOON SHIFT

Carol had nipples too big
for the pasties, brown aureoles
bordering bright silver centers.

CC's G-string had been known to slip,
furred V tucked thick with bills,
lap dances forbidden when plain-clothes
cops came in for their weekly bust.

They left empty-handed,
pants pockets bulging.

Carol was buxom, a tall dark beauty
with just the right shimmy.
Even the women stuffed money
under her glittering belt.

CC's tits were so firm and upright
they could hold a cowboy hat
while she danced, jiggling
out front like a side-saddled filly.

And could she ever skin that dance pole
all the way up and down.
Eye-witness account: *When Coyote Carol*
got done dancing, it looked like the pole
had a new coat of varnish.

Hard to believe where she is these days,
Relief Society president in the Seventeenth
Ward, Latter Day Saint with a past.

JULY WESTHALE

SEX WORK

Dearest,
although all words have passed
over a dark sea, over bronze
urchins with their hands
in their zippers, nothing
has come through me
without your face on it.
Garters lay in cursive.
The name of Magdalene is called,
spat, heaped with dirty silks
growing bitter and cold
against twenty-dollar bills.
You never write, and the road
is lonesome.
All right, I think,
and pulse incurably
and writhe in a hula-hoop
with damp panties, misted
before I go on stage by a spray-bottle
filled with gin. We call this *love.*

AMANDA JOHNSTON

IT AIN'T PROSTITUTION

If you don't take cash
If we're in a recession
If you're married to the trick
If the cutoff notice came
If it was only one time
If he/she was nice
If it was for food
If you didn't kiss
If you know their mama
If it's in another state
If you like it
If you lie like you like it
If you hope they like it
If it's for tuition
If it's for books
If your baby needs school clothes
If you need new clothes
If the rent is due
If you don't go all the way
If you pray about it
If you tithe ten percent
If you change the sheets
If you wash yourself in hot water
If you sleep at night
If you dream
If you need it
If you want it
If you don't remember it

ALCHEMIST

The woman next door says she don't
have to ask if it was me or him
rearranging the furniture last night.

Don't take that much to grow
a man the way you want him.

She tells me how all a woman
had to do to snag her the right man
or cure one from being a terror,
was to scare up some nightshade.

She says it used to be simpler
when the world was simpler.

Used to be in the South, you could
find it just about anywhere on account
of how liberal the law was with hanging men.

You'd look for the mandrake right where
he'd been hung and spasmed the last
of his seed into the earth.

But, she doesn't say, *spasmed his seed.*
She says something else which means
having an orgasm as you die.

You had to harvest the plant before dawn
on a Friday and you'd sometimes
get a four-foot root already bulging
into a homunculus.

But she doesn't say, *homunculus.*
She uses a racial slur.

Then it'd want feeding.
Goat's milk.
Honey.
Dried mushroom.
Blood from a fresh cut.

Eventually that little thing would come
to life, start moving around, wail
like an infant if it didn't have its food.

When it got adolescent-old
you'd slit its throatroot
because, after all, it's just a plant.

Dry it out.
Grind it down.
Serve it in tea to the man
you're wanting to do right and that was that.

What do you do now, I want to know,
if you don't have a mandrake?

She says, *Find someone who do.*
I know where a whole mess of 'em grow.

ELIZABETH COHEN

I PUT A SPELL ON YOU VERSION 2.0

Because I had a red pickup truck
and you were restoring a camper

Because we both loved the color
of October, soaked in wine

Because you smelled like soap
I had long forgotten

Because we accidentally touched
elbows under the lip of the diner counter

Because you liked apricots
and I had some in my refrigerator

Because you came from a wolf
and I came from a canyon

And we both had
new black boots

I cast this spell, on you,
and make you mine.

MARSHA MATHEWS

THE WOMAN WHO ISN'T HIS WIFE

The woman who isn't his wife
shouts words
that should only be whispered,

>   "Doc says he ain't got much time."

The patient's startled eyes
rise up like axes
before shutting down.
His body pulls air
one more time.

Machines gurgle.

His hand jerks.

Now the loud, labored breathing,
is hers.

>   "We met at the diner in Norton,
>   sat on silver stools that twirled
>   while we drank Cherry Coke-a-Colas.
>   Horses clopped the streets. Those days
>   men, their faces black with coal, walked
>   about, chewing tobacco. Had to make
>   a law against spitting on the sidewalk.
>
>   Years later, the booze got him.
>
>   Tried so hard to change him.
>   Tried so hard to love him.
>   Tried so hard to leave him."

Nurses buzz doctors.
Blue masks, swift moves.

> The woman who is not
> supposed to be here
> handkerchiefs his brow
>
> one last time
> slips out
> before the legal wife slips in.

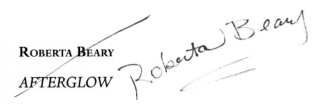

ROBERTA BEARY

AFTERGLOW

rose petal saké—
my crazy is not
his crazy

jasmine scent of the other woman is me

daymoon
grass stains
of original sin

broken vow the gin bottle's vacant blue

the way he says
consensual
mauve sunset

ELLEN BASS

IN PRAISE OF FOUR-LETTER WORDS

We yell *shit*
when the egg carton slips
and the ivory globes
splatter on blue tile.
And when someone leaves you
bruised as a dropped pear, you spit
that fucker, fucking bastard, motherfucker.
And if you just got fired, the puppy
swallowed a two-inch nail, or
your daughter needs another surgery,
you might walk around murmuring
fuckfuckfuckfuckfuck
under your breath like reciting a rosary.

Cock and *cunt*—we spew them out
as though they were offal,
that vulnerable bare skin
of the penis, that swaying it does
like a slender reed in a pond, the vulva
with its delicate mauve or taupe
or cinnamon fluted petals.
You'd think we despise
the way they slide together,
can't bear all those nerves
bunched up close as angels
seething on the head of a pin.

And *suck,* our *yes*
to the universe, first hunger, whole
mammalian tribe of damp newborns
held in contempt for the urgent rooting,

the nubbly feel of the nipple in the mouth,
fine spray on the soft palate.

When life cracks us
like a broken tooth,
when it wears us down
like the tread of old tires,
isn't this what we cry for?
To bring another's body
into our body, whether through our mouths
or that other mouth—to be taken in?

Maybe all that shouting
is shouting to God, to the universe,
or *anyone* who can hear us.
In lockdown within our own skins
we're banging on the bars with tin spoons,
screaming in the only language strong
enough to convey the shock
of our shameful need—the pissing,
cocksucking animal of me begging
to the crapping, cunt-licking animal of you.
Fuck!—we look around us
in terrified amazement—
God damn! God damn! Holy shit!

III.

LYNNELL EDWARDS

FROM: "SUITE FOR WIVES"
I. ME, THE WIFE: VERSIONS OF MEDUSA

One day it will come to this:

Me, in the cave
of our kitchen,
flexing and wet,
music so loud
the walls throb, me
slicing meat
with the biggest knife
you've ever seen,
for a devil stew
you're afraid to eat,
certain I've chopped up
the children or worse. Or

me, upstairs, in our dark
bedroom, eyes
drifting and mystic,
candle and incense smoke
throat-choking thick, me
stammering prophecy
from the great omphalos
of our bed: every way
in is also a way out.
Evidence of ropes, every
nail a different color. Or

me, instead, outside
ground down into the brown
earth of our garden,
chanting for rain and shaking

the root bone of a white rose,
my face bruised
and streaked, my hair
clotted with weeds.

And when it does,
get the mirror,
the reflective shield,
oh my clever Perseus,
even the flat side
of your shining sword.
But do not look upon this;
you will not live to tell.

II. LOVE, HELEN

> All Greece hates
> the still eyes in the white face,
> the luster as of olives
> where she stands,
> and the white hands.
>
> —H.D., "Helen"

A thousand fucking ships
to recover my sweet ass?
What fools. And that's not
the half of it. Listen, bitch:
I wanted out. Out
of that palace house, prison
of Spartan glint and despair;
out from under the sexless
slump of the old man,
his stale breath, palsied grip;
out from the clutches
of the brats we begot, immortals'
burden to issue heirs. Out
of it all, sister. So when
that fine shepherd showed
his sweet face, the swan
in me lifted to meet his mouth,
wild bird heart swollen
like a sail in the Aegean breeze,
his hands on the arc
of my cygnet neck, his hands
sculpting the hollow of my waist,
now winged love soaring

across the waves, the wine-dark
flush of desire unconstrained,
now my marble silence
tightening as a noose
around Troy's breath. And you
want to know why and how
much and when.

I say: take your goddamn thousand ships,
rattling songs of arms and the man,
clarion gifts that seethe revenge,
but know this: when the long battle
years wage on and you wait
for your man while age bends
your brittle frame, spots
your once-milky skin, thins
your fertile hair where he buried
his tears, released his joy,
know this: I am beautiful
still; your men, all dead.

III. JUNO, HER RIVAL

"But the vengeance of Juno was not yet satiated. She sent a gadfly to torment Io, who fled over the whole world from its pursuit."

—Bullfinch's Mythology

I know your dreams, lithe
Io, the dangerous
ones. Domestic, complete,
I know how you imagine
he clothes, feeds you,
how you would perch, flushed,
on the counter in my kitchen
wearing his white shirt,
clever in the crook
of your hooked arms,
bent knees. You watch him
crush garlic with oil,
take his offering, the crust
from his fingertips,
the wine to your lips, meat
from the shining blade.

You would recline
in the swing on the wide,
planked porch, wearing
his work boots, happy
in the rock and sway,
arms extended as he brings
dahlias, roses, asters, lilies
chopped from my garden. Or

most subtle treachery
of all, you are faint
from heat or storm of fever
and to soothe he fashions
schoolboy's verses: how
dear the blush and fumble
when he reads the ink-fresh lines.

But to hide this
deception, he must
bloat the soft hollows
of hip and thigh
where he rests his head,
lays his soft hands,
sprout you horns
at crazed angles from
a head that lolls
on a loose and fleshy neck.
And you will curse
the short rope of tail,
knotted with filth and hair

that swats a black gnat
I have sent to bite
your patched and mange-scarred
flank, spur you
eternally displaced, damned
in your animal stagger to madness.

IV. TROPHY

> I have done with tears. I will endure my death.
>
> —Cassandra, from *Agamemnon*

Aeschylus' Oresteia
Agamemnon, baby, hot
from acquisition, trade,
splendid astride your plunder,
speed me across
the wine-dark lake
in your terrible vessel.
Gilt me as you will:
I am your morning glory, daylily,
bikini-clad figurehead
wedged in the thrust
of a cigarette-sleek bow.
Burden my limbs
with stones the color
of bone and blood.
Buy me a ring
that will cut and shine.
Gun us past the deep channel,
the sheer cliff, the lesser
men in their lesser crafts.
Shred the wake
into white madness,
cutting spray. Agamemnon,
sweetheart, outrace the dark horizon,
thunderheads gnarled
with the surging storm.
Carry me heaving and damp

to your marble halls.
So what you do not hear
my cry above the whine
and saw of horsepower,
the smack of wave against
the hull? So what if
the clattering boast
of other men's gold
shutters the arc of my wail?
So you do not know
the brutal truth of my possession—
the flash of cloaked knife,
the end in nets and slaughter—
the ride, Agamemnon
darling, wasn't it a ride?

MARILYN KALLET

CIRCE, DID YOU?

Circe, like those siren sisters you warned of,
did you croon men to your shore?
Did you surround-sound sailors with silky hair
and nipples? *Oooh,* when you stroked them
with syllables, did it matter to your tongue
who they were? Or were you waiting for one,
Odysseus, with his many-skilled fingers?
In the ruby-tipped dawn did you hold out
for the master mariner, craving mutual song?
Had you dreamed his lure of black hair,
called out his snake-charmer's name, long after
you had previewed that shaggy-dog ending?

Sometimes names trick us into dreams
of having. Odysseus,
an undercurrent, a squall.
Hurricane Odysseus.
Circe, blown away.

ARACHNE & MEDUSA JUMP ATHENA

And it's about time, ain't it?

That girl always kept up some kind of trouble, always starting up some mess. They say trouble don't last always but with Miss Athena, trouble was a never-ending story. What can I say? Some folks like misery and stress. Athena was that way, always up to no good, like to twist and turn things so that everything was about her. Had a real thing for victimhood. Don't get me started on Athena's tears.

Always got to be the finest one in the room. If you didn't know, you better ask somebody. Can't let nobody else shine. See you beaming, she gon' shade and block the sun. See you sipping cool waters, she gon' steal the drops off your thirsting tongue. Athena got to have the last taste— and hers better be sweeter. Or she gon' dry the well with barren sand, and ram the river with a bitter dam. Poison is what she was. Killjoy, ain't got a single sister friend, the first. Only thing worse than a jealous heart is a wounded mind, evil enough to act on it.

First, she see Arachne, my right side, my *bestest* friend, minding her own natural business, weaving like she do. Spinning nothing but love. Arachne spins you dreams you want to follow, braid your whole life through. Hope in every glistening thread and strand, her splendid tapestries the work of a master's hand. But Athena can't stand to see nobody else's beauty but her own. She see mine and tried to take it. Thought a head full of snakes would erase it. Talking 'bout, *see who gon' want you now.*

Hmpf. Athena always been simple minded. Her aim is sure, but her vision unclear. She see what she want to see and what she want is pain. Seem like everywhere she gaze, she see lack in herself, instead of looming possibility. She thinks beauty is what you see. She never bothered to look inside, to seek within, or she would know beauty is not where you've been, it's where you're going. Beauty is what you be.

So Arachne and me come up with a master plan. Athena was always terrorizing the land, ripping and running so, through the woods taking lives with her tainted arrows. Talking 'bout, *bow down to the queen.* We wait 'til she deep dark in the woods. We wait 'til she can't see her way out, 'til she standing right where we stood. Arachne spins a web so pretty, it look like starlight, like great heaven above moonshine. A great silver mirror, glistening and shimmering in the shadowy night, even the fireflies stop blinking and hover in the hushed air, admiring its light.

Athena stops to stare. Now, she's the one that started that whole *mirror, mirror on the wall, fairest one of them all* mess, ratchet folks been trying it ever since. While she stunting and staring, Arachne's magic threads reflect the huntress' best self. I sneak out from my hiding place behind the elder tree, unwrap my hair 'cuz now it's *all eyes on me.*

We leave Athena there, a century or two, frozen in her vanity. Arachne gathers her webs and threads. I retie my headwrap and don my shades, while we laugh and laugh, dragging her name behind us in the dust.

GALATEA ALONE

I have grown accustomed to his hands,
the rough palms on my knees, the cracked thumbs
still caked with plaster making their demands,
circling my thigh until it's numb.

And I have grown accustomed to his praise.
I stand before his friends, unpin my hair,
arrange my arms, and lower my gaze
so he can boast that no one else compares.

But I am still adjusting to the feeling
that these long limbs are more than a display.
(The velvet of my skin can send me reeling
when I bathe!) Oh, Venus, let him stay

out late, tell his stories, drink his wine.
Tonight, let this body be all mine.

GREGORY L CANDELA

PAEAN: MAN IN THE MOON

Apollo thrust Neil Armstrong
onto the moon's face
(at moon-faced Jack's behest)
to take one small step for a man.

But neither poet nor president
put any man in the moon.
Dionysus, the mad Mediterranean
transvestite, has no power there.

Men are skulls, sutured
tectonics. Hard head bones
that sweat and grow restless
mean beneath the full moon.

Diana tears continents apart
shifts glandular tides and
siphoned Lee Harvey Oswald up
the book depository stairs
drew Apollo's Armstrong into
her arms and pieces of bone
and brain out through
poor Jack's shattered face.

The moon has. no. horns.
Look at her pelvic wings
ample for laying eggs. Dare
look squarely into her round
face, half-lidded, moist bedroom
eyes, supplicant, pouty lips.

Listen—sad misfit Marilyn
always about to sing—
happy birthday, mr. president.

RUTH FOLEY

DAPHNE

I spend my days staring at my hair, willing
it to burst into leaf—it is autumn, and trees
are smoldering. I would kindle, too, here
away from you where if I light it is my still
and only burning. I'm told my skin is done
already—maybe that can be a sign of coming
bark. Or maybe I should tell you not to think
about its silk or scent. If we both refuse to move,

perhaps we can become substantially rooted,
separate. I will grasp essential lies: I don't need
your worship or your care. I don't need to be
stripped, laureled on your victorious head.
Some days I wonder what is lost if we surrender.
If only you would ruin me, I could be ruined.

JESSICA D. THOMPSON

DIANA
Slade, Kentucky ca. 1975

In her dreams, she sees rabbits
running in the woods.

White ones swallow black
ones, head first and whole.

She labors to push them out
before they stop

breathing. In her mind,
she has infinite children

with cherub faces.
They bring her what they kill.

She eats the hearts first,
before they go bad—

            as all hearts will.

LAUREL DIXON

DELILAH RUNS WITH SCISSORS

The curls are black against her fingers,
one fistful of darkness delivered
to the highest bidder, silver scissors
clutched in her opposite hand.
She leaves Samson sleeping,
his face cragged and cracked
with that ancient trust. The lawn
is slick and thick with dew, her legs
pumping in a stumble-rhythm away
from the house where they lived.

Her mother always said:
If you get out, girl, get out fast.
Samson, when you wake
mortality will smear
across your face like lipstick—
your strength gone, only
your swift silver temper
left to burn.

MARTA FERGUSON

ORACLE COMPLAINS ABOUT THE JOB

Goddess! Some days I want to crack
their shapely skulls together and have
done with it. Crime-fighting may be
worthwhile, but sitting here on the
administrative end of every fight or flight
in town, yow! I may as well be routing toys
for Santa. Less stress, no greater complications.

And I never get OUT, I'm too *valuable*
to the team. I know what that means.
Go back to the lab, Bones. Work that sexy brain.
Yeah, yeah. But for the record, my kung fu beats
your kung fu any day of the week.

Though I've been stuck in here long enough
I'm not quite sure which day that is.

ALISON STONE

PERSEPHONE RETURNING

I was no stolen child.
I chose to grab the hundred-blossomed flower,
to pull until earth opened like a woman
and the moss became my bridal veil.

My body swelled.
Pluto split the bloody fruit
and fed me sweetness.
We wove our bones together
on the clammy ground.

Now at my step
the cold earth blooms
and sex commands its dance.
Returned, I skip among the buds.
Mother takes me in her leafy arms.
But the animals know—
beneath my girlish face,
a queen who dipped her feet
into the lake of death.
I am both deserting daughter
and abandoned mother holding back the rain.
Mine are the dark mysteries,
mine, too, the secret of the grain

DAN SICOLI

AND WE LAY BY THE WATER'S EDGE FOR DAYS, OUR SKIN NEARLY EVOLVING

i.

once the mermaid walked out of the sea
      politicians jockeyed for a photo-op
      young children giggled and hid behind skirts
      old men ogled
      priests closed their worried eyes

a revision from the sea
      she walked tailless
      upright
      leaving confident footprints in damp sand

as droplets casually fell from
      her body to earth
      residents wondered what
      would sprout there

the day the mermaid abandoned her gown of water
      a young daughter scurried to her
      and placed one star below her breast
      neptune was appeased

ii.

the day the mermaid arrived
      we finally realized
      there'd be no cure for darwin
      accepting her unconditionally

convinced she had come to share knowledge
        to whisper secrets of her body
        the elders became advocates
        enticed by her light
        as teacher not deity

schoolchildren were fascinated
        by her draping scarlet hair
        as it nearly swept the ground
        she walked

iii.

still some insisted she was goddess
        scribes busied themselves
        categorizing names and titles given her
        inventing logic to make them all fit

she waved off their allegiance
        instead instructing them
        on how to breathe in two realms
        and how to measure time
        by the weight of water

from confidence sprung arrogance
        they no longer respected water's edge
        believing they had been chosen
        some drowned in their own breath

iv.

often in darkness
>she dreams of dwelling
>in her once-abandoned home
>wistful, perhaps, for the chains
>of its refuge

days burdened themselves under their own mass
>and she too grew heavy
>pining for
>her previous owner

her primordial instinct intensified
>for a solace she once knew
>even with withered fins
>the hunger continued

once atop the bulb of the county water tower
>she stood naked at the rim
>holding her dress limply in arms
>then allowing it to swirl to earth

leaping off as full wings sprouted
>from bare shoulders
>she soared into a gaze of buoyant eyes
>into a new dress of clouds
>as the star ignited from her breast

SHERYL HOLMBERG

ANIMA MUNDI

The snake sheds her skin in a circle
waiting for the pattern
to re-emerge, calmly turning
back upon herself in movement and in sleep
scant regards the mosaic she carries, tale of eternal serpent
legends of a younger world
another time, of Rainbow Serpent carrying the world
coiled beneath in perfect circling
slumber, undisturbed the serpent
dreams, the pattern
of days and nights weave through her sleep
as over and under the sky is turning
wheeling around the earth is turning
she dreams the world
snaking songlines singing sleep
and the circle
is drawn, the pattern
follows mosaic on the back of the serpent
as she slides into dreams like Kukulcan, the winged serpent,
descending the staircase, Mayan calendar turning
on the equinox, fulfilling the pattern
of rain falling over the world
creating rainbows circling
past horizons, past lines of sight, the rhythms of sleep
drumming from drops of light singing to sleep
the serpent
coiled in her perfect colors, the circle
of time is turning
throwing shadows, sewing seasons as the world
wheels on, spinning its pattern
of green and blue, oceans of water encircled in patterns

of siren snakes asleep
and singing, weaving the world
out of her dreams, in soft slumber Celestial Serpent
weaving sun and stars through the turning
sky as night and day meet in a circle
perfect as the pattern on the serpent's
back, mosaic shifting as she sleeps, turning
over and over with the world, dreaming a perfect circle.

PENELOPE KARAGEORGE

MANHATTAN CIRCE

Observe, please, that Circe, the enchantress, is enisled,
   drawing a big watery ring around herself,
island lady with magic that turns men into swine
   but mostly makes them more like men.

And as they rediscover their masculine powers,
   they begin to forget Circe. Like Odysseus
marking the days until he'd return home to
   Ithaca where Penelope waited.

And how amazed Penelope would be, putting down her knitting,
   turning off the TV to make love, thrilling
to the new Odysseus, while Circe weeps alone. She goes
   to other goddesses for advice

but they revel in her grief, won't tell her the rules.
   So she's stuck with men who love her, but leave
her. If she could live in a white house, she'd reinvent
   herself, take the island steamer home,

find a lover she could keep and keep, wear him like
   a diamond, showing his picture on every
occasion, treat him like a king, opening packets of sugar for
   his coffee, break their teeth with his fidelity.

She wants potholders and things that match. Her silver
   chairs are tarnished. There are cracks
in the walls of her stone palace. The terrace leaks.
   The rent keeps going up; she cannot pay the price.

And each time a lover leaves she must remix the potions,
conjure up the magic once again. Do they know
how hard it is? Harder and harder, and how sometimes
now, despite Circe's powers, it does not work.

HILA RATZABI

SEDNA THE ARCTIC SEA GODDESS

The men fashioned their bitch goddess into a fat girl.
Daughter of Anguta, creator-god, angry dad.

In every legend your father throws you to sea.
You cling to kayak: he cuts off your fingers.

You drown. Your fingers become seals, walruses, whales,
Creature-fingers sprung from sea-blood.

You leash your seals
Hold back fish in your silky palm

Till the hunters hunger so much they send shamans
To wash and comb your hair.

Only a man's goddess would lose use of her hands.
Only a man's goddess would withhold food in exchange for praise.

No wonder you rage at the bottom of the sea.
No wonder you explode with hurricanes when man's heat

Sends you to a frenzy and you shake
Your stump of a fist at dry land.

ANDREW MERTON

CRUISE SHIP INTERVENTION

God wakes from Her nap
in one of Her moods,

just in time to change the tide.
She puts on a rhinestone-studded jumpsuit,

purple stilettos, lipstick,
slings a boa around Her shoulders

and struts out on deck.
She's gorgeous, if you like that sort of thing.

And, admit it, pal, you do.
Yes you, in the faded blue blazer,

staring over the railing,
working up the courage to jump.

I'd turn around if I were you.
Can't you feel the current shifting?

SOSHA PINSON

GOD-THE-MOTHER TO MOSES AFTER THE CROSSING

This will not happen again.
My sea limbs spread for you
to enter with his "chosen" people.

Even when you slit that throbbing vein
of a river in Egypt and summoned blood
from me, I felt you tremble.

Yes, like any woman, I bleed.

Do you think with the force
of a rod you can have
whatever you please?

It was him who coaxed me, called the name
I used to be worshipped by—*Asherah,*
it'll be like old times, remember? Just do this for me.

Don't forget my murmurs lulled you to sleep
in case you were to cry & be found
your reeded arc flipped, infant body flailing

against my current, helpless like each of Pharaoh's
militiamen once he slammed my knees shut, saying *finished*
saying *let them drown*

as if everything that he dams inside me
dies. He doesn't know the story of destroyed
people: they adapt. He is not

the only life-bringer.

EMILY LEIDER

ARGUING WITH A GODDESS

A crudely made small Venus figurine
Glass-cased at Les Eyzies
Carved out of stone or bone or tusk.
Cave-creature, amulet.
Her torso thick, earth-forced
Breasts bursting like two laden boughs,
Her rump a gnarl.
All one big lump or hump
To pillow thrusts and saddle births.
But it's the face that galls:
She has none.

STACEY BALKUN

LILITH

after "Lilith" (1892) by John Collier

She's so pale I doubt she's breathing. The sharp lynchpin
of her waist dips inward as if her torso and hips

were a switchback on a trail, two directions
on the same path. Where is her gooseflesh?

How can her hair be so smooth? Once, I stood naked
in a forest, just at the edge of the trees, looking down

at the ocean and the rest of Big Sur, the orange hoods

of California poppies lit like small fires in the underbrush.
I shivered and pulled tangles and twigs

from my hair after lying with a man under the redwood trees.
Let's say he left me there. It's true, he was frightened

by a garter snake. Let's say Lilith, tornado-woman,

just furied Adam. This is about something untouchable,
something I'm trying to understand about poppies

a jug of water, the rough mulch.

The serpent wraps her in his shining skin like a man's
arms and she hugs him closer, arches her back, legs pressing

together to hide the scallop-shaped blood mirrored on her thighs.

ANDROMEDA WAS BLACK IS BEAUTIFUL AS A SUITE
(for bass clarinet and bass)

I.

a sound apart chained to rock, prepare to meet
your end starchild. breakers crush against boogie
that cymbal crash that lonely is a sea. a sinking ship
breaks like this sound done wandered into deep
waters, into some unlikelihood, some mythical
unlikeliness of that eritrean chick nobody could jump off tonal even
with the whole western canon in the pocket.

II.

those issues of scope are not hers so modal. her entirely
original movements and what she has and what you lost that's how
she dare get all the sun she need from the moon. the interrupture be
a beautiful black woman is a beautiful curse. did her damnedest was
vibes the whole world melody got black mama issues to. like water
for chocolate skin squashed the paper bag test, and then her stylish
broadway took the cakes home to cake more accordingly.

the intermezzi. the jump is jointin'. the numinous obliques. the purlieu.
the shade thrown off. the hustle. the good good. the linger under the
moon. the flesh's offices. the rent. the gigue is uptown. the bravura. the
dougie. the monster's ball. the do the damn thing already damn it.

III.

always especially the third movement,

somebody's mama's sista like
a fist full of dap was good
from cuz to see his feet fresh
and every tooth in him mouth
gold on the false. ethiopia is a
real place in her solecism and

gentle and lower registers niccas
cram to understand what's
going on busting out under that
consciousness got 'em feeling
some type of way about the afro
puffiness.

IV.

what is that that just come from the four winds just look at the way it's
codeswitching, oh mercy. but even then, gotta all her own secret body
only she can (sing the lonely hours). hips shaped like emergency as a
singing siren the thang put down, it shook, and broke every potential
awning down to the tuning. holla ata intersectionality was supple and
tore elegance right out the frame way out of the range of the harp.
higher notes. high booty, high john conqueror root in the pocket back.
the most distant object visible to the naked eye is all she wrote (to
attica).

JULY WESTHALE

SALOME

She'd danced in a pen and the price
was small change. With a lion and flames
creating stilted light the circus makes
but does not desire. The mirrors
full of nudity, and the tent blown up
like a skirt, men spending to catch
all that fire, agape mouths the size
of areolas or dinner platters that had seen
feast, famine, fortune, heads.

You ever met a girl with such big
hopes, with so costly a ticket, and the moon
hanging in double-vision along her collar?

Her neck is a road anyone would travel home.

NOAH'S ENDANGERED SPECIES

You enter a dark room. All the women you've loved sit at a candlelit
table: Holly, such a firecracker, she exploded

the room. Before vodka washed away her spark, she clawed a white
firework into your shoulder, tore

your beard when you said, *you're like your mom,* then went shooting
off with another man like a Roman candle.

Sandy, the marathon runner, chased a river of Wild Turkey
with a bottle of Seconal when you ended

the relationship at its finish line; Olive, the lounge singer with legs like
Tina Turner, who battered

both your heart and hers. Your cherubic high school girlfriend
whose mother staggered in the door, eyes

aglitter with gin. Leered at you on the couch, said, *I'm a Pecker-Checker.*
Though you tried to pull

her daughter from her raging genetic squall, years later, on the phone,
still, you heard her drowning. She rose

like a damp angel when cancer swathed her in a gray cloak—
Now, in these shadows, you trace each female silhouette.

The waterfall of a shoulder surges into a long neck. Like giraffes, those
women drank from love's well in a world

flooded by cruel humans. Aren't they human? They could've migrated,
fought back, learned to adapt

to the cold. You've evolved into a man who loves the same woman.
Learned to speak without your voice

thundering over her. Now: question marks whirlpool beneath
your eyelids. Their eyelashes

like Venus flytraps, swat away gadflies. Stop pulling them
into your rickety arc. They don't want a partner

who won't sink. Turn off the light. Come to bed. All you can do, love,
is pray for a world that's as warm and awake as you.

K. Nicole Wilson

EVE WAS THE ORIGINAL CATCHER

Licking chocolate off the sharp edges of a serrated knife
is worth the risk,
it's better to eat cake than be a wife,
guarding the plate like Carlton Fisk

is worth the risk.
If the pitching's distressed,
guarding the plate like Carlton Fisk
is useless,

if the pitching's distressed,
cleaning the dish
is useless—
a dustless world is just a wish.

Cleaning the dish
leaves time for contemplation:
a dustless world is just a wish,
total happiness is an imagination,

leave time for contemplation,
don't obsess,
total happiness is an imagination,
just try to minimize the mess,

don't obsess,
it's better to eat cake than be a wife,
just try to minimize the mess,
licking chocolate off the sharp edges of a serrated knife.

NICHOLAS SAMARAS

EVE NAMING OTHER ANIMALS

Slender horns approach, and I find
my touch makes them shapely: fronds

of opaque light that dance from angles.
I like their intimacy more than angels,

more than that shimmer that stays in place.
Into the meadow of limbs and motion, I trace

the bent wheat to be with them there.
Like a gesture moving through air,

it is a gesture moving through air.
I find this given language spare,

suddenly. It leaves too soon in breath.
Fellow creatures, I take the fenneled path

of you. The glance of our forms
in our reflective eyes. Our terms

for each other—need they be so ruled
and firm? The he-me: boredom I've hurled

at your feet, your white gait flinting
the light. I name you "event cantering."

That one I call "this for now" because it unfolds
and folds and, furry, crimps away. And, behold,

you, yellow-wrinkling the leaf-tailed grasses—
I name you "shape of you," that, muscled, passes

under the thrilling shiver of your skin.
I name you "changeable wish," and let you in

to this space of myself to contain largeness,
to hold and let go of moments words should caress.

I name you "fire dancing in mouth." Excite
me with stories. Stroll me back in the night

and call me, too. "Feathers folding" fly
down to trees. Backsided, the light walks away.

ALISON TOWNSEND

GOSPEL OF JESUS'S WIFE REVEALED TO BE PROBABLE FAKE

But think if this tattered bit of papyrus
the size of a credit card, splashed huge
in a two page spread in *The Atlantic,* were real.
Hand-lettered, each word in what appears
to be Coptic caps, it looks more like something
stenciled on the side of a burlap feedbag
than a sacred text, gospel that could change
the course of Christian thought.
But who wouldn't want to believe,
the words terse and fragmentary
as if torn from a poem—*my wife she is able*
to be my disciple and *I am with her in order to*—
for the way they let us enter another realm,
opening the way through the world of men,
neatly as the part in Mary Magdalene's hair.

Which must have seemed a river
as he stared down at her, washing his feet
with salt from her own body, then drying them
with its tangled red gold, the gesture
not abased but tender, so gentle something
in him stirred, lonely in this business
of performing miracles, sick of his role
as the son of God. Think of him, leaning
toward her, placing his hands on her head,
the silk of it drawing him in like a dream
of butter and honey and sun, a whirlpool
that, if we are lucky, swallows us all
at least once or twice in a lifetime.

As for what happened next, who can say.
But she knew something he needed to know
and he knew it. This isn't the story
the Apostles tell, but something deeper, darker,
more human—a story of flesh and bone and blood,
the story of a woman at the foot of the cross,
she who hurried bravely to the tomb at first light—
the one for whom, perhaps, he was really resurrected.

LAUREN BOISVERT

SCHEHERAZADE

Roses in my hair, my body is a stiff stone wall
where fists beat like angry winds, mad birds bloody
against the windows. They fall at my mercy. I show them none.
I am a queen, swords for hands, a thousand and one tales
in my four-chambered heart.

Ribbons in my hair, my body is a tall stone house
that burns inside with red demon fire. My spine
is an alignment of planets that starts a war in the heavens.
My mouth is that war brought to earth.

Rivers in my hands, my body is a hard stone fence
running the edge of the woods. My breath is a fog
that smothers the mounds of many dead kings.
My thoughts are trees that stretch and die. I am an impossible being
made possible by belief: the goddess on her throne,
the devil in his burning halls.

I appear gentle and soft as new snow but my blood is thick as ichor.
My body is a siege tower, my mind is breaking machinery.

Look to your cities, your stories, your lovers.
I am coming for them all. My night will never end.

Jeremy Paden

TECUICHPOTZIN

How many husbands can one woman survive?
Betrothed, once barely weaned, to a man killed
by Cortés. Taken then by an uncle,
at ten, to secure his right to the throne.
And he dead within days from Spanish pox.
Then cousin Cuahtémoc, an eagle swooping
down on the cactus of empire, clasped you,
his bride, in his talons, only to be hung
on some tree in some southern jungle
by Cortés. Seventeen and given as wife,
again, now a Spaniard—hand and body,
given, with Tecuba city, Tecuba
lands, Tecuba Indians, as dowry.
And he soon dead. Then brought for protection
into Cortés until expectant. Wed off
now to a man who would raise a girl named
Cortés Moctezuma and not complain.
Another death, another head of house,
before the cloister and the veil, the vows
and that final Husband who let you be
until he too came, at last, to take your life.

BIANCA BARGO

OPHELIA

I.

Green was always her favorite color.
To her it was alive and thriving,
blooming and growing,
young and hopeful,
as she was once.

She wanted to go where the green was and
float beneath the surface-skimming limbs,
beside the mossy banks and the
tall, firm reeds.

She knew she herself had been too green.
She believed his love-soaked promises.
She let his fickleness and treachery
fuel her own fall into
madness.

So she donned a dress in her favorite color,
plucked a fist's flowers from the
feathery grass to take with her
to the water, and she let all
the green in her world
fade slowly
into black.

II.

In the evenings of my younger days,
I'd fill the tub a little less
than halfway

and lower myself back
into the soothing heat,
arms braced
left and right.
I'd let all my hair get wet
and fan it out gently all around
me so I could look over and see
the soft strands ripple and surge
beneath the steamy surface.

Now it makes me think of her.
I'm sure her hair looked beautiful
splayed all about her in the water,
floating out from her smooth brow
and long neck, in swirls around her
shoulders, reaching out to the banks,
clouding up the surface—
I'm sure she probably didn't notice.

III.

You should have stuck it out, Ofi.

You should've gritted your teeth
and hummed those eerie songs
to yourself.

You should have harbored all the hurt and
let it smolder beneath your breast.

You should have clenched your fists till
your fingernails left your palms bloody.

You should have hoisted up the hem of your dress
and run for a front-row seat at the final scene
so you could have seen the Danish Prince
who sent you drowning
get his in the end.

BARBARA CROOKER

SNOW WHITE TURNS SIXTY

and doesn't care any
more about what the neighbors
think. The prince just
sits there, in his recliner,
flicking channels, popping
brewskis. Belches. He got down-
sized last year from The Royal
Kingdom. Too young
for social security; too old
for another career. She just
doesn't care. They haven't touched
in years. The kids are grown,
the house runs itself, and who wants
to go to another ball or support
another charity? She's into:
yoga, organic gardening, book club.
She's highlighting her hair, lifting
weights, feels better about her body
than she has in years. She sees
the future roll out ahead, a road
through the woods in autumn, yellow
leaves scattered on the ground. There
might be a snug little cottage, just for one.
Maybe a cat curled by the chimney, soft
as smoke. And a kettle on for tea.
Pull up a chair and listen. You won't
believe her story.

SHERRY CHANDLER

PUTSCH AND COUNTER PUTSCH

> for six years ... Athaliah ruled the land.
>
> —2 Kings 11:3

Jumping Jehoshaphat, Jehu, did you slaughter
so many to be thwarted by a woman?
Who can fault the lack of thought for daughters'
heads in those seventy baskets? Was no omen

given? Even Jezebel fell—she was putsched—
from the window where she sat to await
her fate, without resistance, makeup fixed,
to face you down before she hit the street.

One thing to Lady-Macbeth it, put the screws
on with the proper weapons, sex and wiles,
another to fight the coup outright, to seize
the throne and stack the bodies up in piles.

That's the prerogative of the righteous male,
prophet-blessed to reap the profits of blood.
Then let the record taint the name Athaliah,
and her intolerable tolerance for the wrong god.

ELIZABETH BURTON

PRAYER FOR THE HUNGRY GHOSTS

You can find her lurking
In front of churches
After the wedding party
Has left, trying to jam
Handfuls of tossed rice
Down her skinny throat.
She won't arrive
Until after the festivities
Have ended. She's already in hell,
So there's no point in forcing
Herself to watch the ceremony.
Scraps of stale love
Taste nothing like the real
Thing, but she gorges
Anyway, first rice,
Then the last few slices
Of wedding cake,
Before the caterers sweep
It away into the trash.
She notes, dimly
(Over the constant rumble
Of fire in her belly),
That what she's doing
Is meaningless,
But she gnaws the head
Off of the tiny plastic bride
For good measure.

KAREN KOVACIK

MUSES OF A CERTAIN AGE

They flee from binoculars, plumage in camouflage, all grays and browns. Stand a full-length mirror in a shorn field, and you'll see only sky, maybe smoke, a scarf of stars. Even their ponds appear still.

It's not enough to slip a bag over your unlined face or go two weeks without sleeping. You must set a glass of red wine in a clearing, load up your iPod with the blues. Then place a splint on your ankle, and try to coax them to dance.

Maybe they'll come bearing quatrains, austere as monks. Maybe they'll want to kiss you or get high. Whatever happens, loosen up. You're in their habitat now.

And if your lack of self-knowledge traps you like honey or amber, they'll swarm to tug you free. Their sheer gowns black with words. Their barbs that smart but won't kill.

SARAH FAWN MONTGOMERY

(UN)SINKABLE

Molly in Missouri, cotton dress sticking
to the back of her dusty, sweaty knees.

Molly on the farm, jumping rope,
collecting eggs and milking cows.

Molly selling perfume behind a counter,
spritzing ladies in big feathered hats.

Molly marrying J.J., singing
Irish songs like their immigrant parents.

Molly making pies—cherry, rhubarb—
spoon-feeding J.J. when he comes home.

Molly wanting to vote,
getting ladies suffragetting.

Molly seeing stars
when J.J. strikes a gold vein.

Molly buying furs, silk gloves,
a big house in Denver.

Molly learning French,
speaking thick Russian.

Molly painting, playing piano.
Molly running for Senate.

Molly wanting, wanting more,
snowy Denver—J.J.—too small now.

Molly first-class Titanic,
sipping whiskey alone.

Molly hears the crack,
feels the great lurching shift.

Molly shouts directions,
hot-blooded despite the ice.

Molly stays last—ship drowning—
three men needed to get her into a lifeboat.

Molly takes command, searching for bodies,
floppy feather in her hat freezing stiff.

Molly at the tiller.
Molly unsinkable.

Molly crying upon return,
waking up alone, choking in the night.

Molly pacing the big house, ice
in her bones, a berg just out of sight.

Molly giving speeches, making rounds,
awards in her shaking hands.

Molly acting onstage:
smile, turn, adjust beaded gown.

Molly seeing things in the wings,
staring out into the dark.

Molly with a headache, seeing stars,
ice, the memory of something pressing in.

Molly with a tumor, the doctor says,
bobbing around the current of her brain.

Molly feeling faint.
Molly sinking to the floor.

FRIDA KAHLO'S SELF-PORTRAIT WITH MONKEY

Animals circle her and settle on her
like lazy whirlwinds and light rebozos
in all her portraits, photos, and home movies.
Monkeys wrap their arms around her shoulders,
their necks collared with the same red
ribbon that entwines her throat.
Another monkey tries to undo
her sharp dark necklace of thorns.
Blue parrots perch on her sleeves and rest
in her purple lap. She embraces
a fawn, and in a brief film clip, it totters
along on her walk, in the shadow of her skirt.

Some friends blamed her pets for her lack
of children. You may not know the theories people hold
and state about how if you only would or would not
do something else, you could bear babies,
no matter the condition of your pelvis.
Let them have their theories. She had
a life of other people's children, dolls,
and near her bed, a pickled fetus in a jar.

ELIZABETH BECK

JOYFUL EXIT

> I was born a bitch. I was born a painter
>
> —Frida Kahlo

Looking like a sunflower
sitting upright, blaze
of fire ring around your
head because cremation
not enough to damp spark
of life that compelled two
hundred paintings savagely
portraying women's pain
because you knew

suffering surgeries and bed-
ridden (although perhaps
you enjoyed the bed), daring
marriage tumultuous passion
tumbling sheets soiled by mis-
carriages too many for one
woman to endure, embracing
existence la vie bohème necessary
until you (perhaps) chose your end

LISA HARTZ

INCANTATION, TRANSLATION
Portrait Of The Herbalist, *Doris Ulmann, Lang Syne Plantation,*
South Carolina, Circa 1929–1931

> This woman appears to be not only of androgynous character but also of
> mixed race. The mystery of her origins and sexuality seems appropriate
> for one who practiced curing and conjuring with the help of herbal
> recipes.
>
> —Judith Keller,
>   Associate Curator of the Department of Photographs,
>   The J. Paul Getty Museum

Leaves, roots, blooms. Heal
the wound. Chase the curse.
Spell it back again.
Mojo hand, conjure bag. Green
flannel for money. White
for baby. I collect the pieces
in the sack according to
your need. Frog eye, honeycomb.
Fingernail, batwing. Orchid root
for lucky hand. Swallow heart
for love. Breathe on it.
Bring it life. Soak it in
whiskey. In piss. In jizz.
Hide it between your skirt
and your sex. It is alive
with spirit. O sinner. O
mourner. There is nothing
between you and this earth.
There is everything between
you and this earth. Fill
the honey jar, put the name
inside. Love cannot resist you now.

IV.

TERRY ANN CARTER

THE WILDEST THING I'VE EVER DONE
IN HONOUR OF MY TRIP TO PARIS

In honour of my visit to Paris
I've decided to name my breasts
Gertrude (the larger one)
and Alice (the smaller)
on the occasion of a literary tour,
which of course will include
their Luxembourg Gardens pied-à-terre.

In the evening when I am bathing
I look down at Miss Toklas, Miss Stein, whisper ...
we're going, we're going to France.
And the larger one wants to hold salons,
invite writers for plum brandy.
The smaller one
wants to eat hash brownies.

Kiki Petrosino

THIGH GAP

It's true: I have
it, though I hardly approve
of anything it does.

Supposed bend of light
or smudge where two odd
angles is—I hardly see

can hardly do a thing
with it. White zone of
no flesh pressing

into no. So low, I can't
scale or measure it. I used
to think: OK, *a clean sharp place*

to keep. And: *I'll grow*
a thing to keep, for me. But
no. It's just a ward

to mark & count, a loop
I lope around with, so
I count

myself a realm
of realms. I vote & vote.
Turns out, we agree

with everything we
does, almost. We sweep
the precincts

of ourself: above, below.
the rooms between
each rib & under them

till finally we reach the fat
red condo where
our blood lights up.

We live here now. Half
ranch, half townhouse in
the chest. Just think

on it. Turn on
that sweet TV. *Mise en place*
a nap, a nook: we're full

of stuff. We paint
the pergola we couldn't
live without. It's true

at last: we have it all
though we hardly know
what any of it does.

TO THE WAY I WALK

O Hips, I haven't always loved
the way you do what you want.
If it were up to me,
you wouldn't be so flamboyant,
but you? You choose to sashay.

People stop me on the street
to comment on your swing.
Bring that bouncy walk over here,
a woman told me last week,
as if I were the one in charge.
You're hypermobile, the yoga teacher says,
a warning disguised as a promise.
What nobody claims is: It don't mean a thing.

But I forgive you, Hips. I've come to love you
like twin daughters. I want to look after you,
because you? you swinging, bouncing, sashaying hips,
you peripatetic pelvis, you ebullient ass?
O sweet thing, O honey chile, it worries me
you don't protect yourself the way you should.

KAREN PAUL HOLMES

ZUMBA WITH LADY GAGA: DIVORCE THERAPY

A week ago, I didn't know Lady Gaga
from Lady Godiva.
Now I'm stumbling through
a fusion of Latin, hip-hop, belly and pop
while Gaga rocks her lyrics right at me:
She still loves her Judas too.
After three Zumba classes I'm keeping up—
salsa, samba, and the Kumbia Kings:
Fuego! The roof's burnin' but we don't care.
Bollywood, calypso, soca, reggaeton
(faster now; heart rate up!)
Step on the *gasolina:* My baby likes *gasolina!*
(or something like that).
I'm told some of the words are dirty—luckily
(or un), I don't know Spanish, Arabic, Hindi
and can't catch half the English.
Panting, we take it down a notch to the lyric
I'm lookin' for a Jack who's not a ripper.
Then: right foot cha cha cha
left foot cha cha cha
turn turn turn turn
        step right
step left
swim, monkey, frugue, pony.
Our 20-ish teacher calls this one "the '80s"
but I recall go-go boots in sixth grade, 1966.
Now it's, "Bring out your inner Beyoncé!"
for *Single Ladies,* the only song I knew before.
More mambo, tango and a peppy meringue rap:
the guy has passion in his pants
and likes to flaunt it.

Miraculously, I can now shimmy.
Mirrors line one wall.
That's me smilin', sweatin', hot
pink tank, black tights—
like the last song says,
I'm groovin' my rock moves
and I don't need
him
tonight.

Karen Kovacik

TO MY LAST PERIOD

For 30 years you muscled onto my calendar
in red ink. And always the week before your arrival

I slept badly, adrift in a lightless fog,
till you showed up and twisted my guts into knots.

Each month you cracked that red whip,
and, baby, I never failed to jump.

So many times I wanted to do myself in
days before you dropped by, but now I guess I'll outlast you:

the widow's revenge. And when you're gone for good,
I'll clean out my closet, flaunt a white skirt and sip

red wine without spilling. I'll dream of grenadine,
kisses of saffron and poppy—but never you.

HILARY SHEERS

STATEMENT

Age has not withered me
Nor custom staled my penumbrate variety
For I am plumper more shaded round the edge
Than I was.
Some thirty pounds of bounded bloomer flesh
About to turn to crepe and shrivel off the bone
Leaving the flesh to hang and shiver
Paper like
Bulk wafers downy breasts
Falling now to greet a gently curving abdomen
Hiding the waste of nights unbedded and lusting
Lips I miss.
Ocean of life lapping in my wake
Heading south while I am steered to Arctic Pole
Deceiving desert blanched late unsullied waist
Look for holes
For fishing, dangle lines where frosted water bumps
And nudge an iceberg to the warming stream
Where age old meets old age and lust love meets
Its pension.

DEBRA WOOLLEY

A NOTE ABOUT THE GIRL WHO RUINED MY WEDDING

Well, *ruined* is a strong word, but that's what my mother would call it. And I have the pictures to prove it. About three-quarters drunk on cab, her favorite drink, a leftover taste from the Red Wine Diet that got her back to 108 lbs only weeks after her daughter was born. I blame the dress. Here we were at the banquet hall of the Signature Grand, and the dress kept falling down, and by the time the band started playing her jams, she'd had enough, and spreading her legs papsmear-wide, grabbed the slippery folds, hiked them up and over her thighs and started to move, her arms jutting, legs kicking, and I stood and watched the buck and swirl and dip and sway of the sage satin bridesmaids dress it took me months to decide on. Her silver slippers lay to the side of the dance floor like wounded soldiers on a battlefield. Yes, you could call it dancing. Formlessly. Dead to rule and rote. In a minute, the folds would slip from her grasp as she tried to hike them higher, onlookers aghast/intrigued, getting a glimpse of her lacy white underwear as she continued, limbs now a great spectacle of discord; her body, a piece of jazz, wild and beautiful.

Victoria Sullivan

BARBWIRE GIRLS

barbwire girls skin their knees
bless the earth with thighs
splayed across moist grass
t-shirts tied at belly and sleeve
hair glazed with moonlight
midnight sweat

keep stag-handled knives
nestled in pockets too small
tube of lipstick, cheap lighter
pressed against pelvic bone

wrap themselves in metal
thorn, braid it through belt loops—
keeps the coyotes away

DIANE KENDIG

BASHA TEACHING BALADY

i. Introductions

"It's not, 'belly,' it's 'balady,'
no hootchy kootchy. No show
a child couldn't see. I have two rules:
no boobs shook in anyone's face,
no tricks with money.

ii. Back Snake Lesson

A serpent in front of a waterfall
or a slinky toy with no strings attached.
It takes guts to be this spineless,
But your spine's been holding you up
all day. This is what you do for your spine.

iii. Sword Dance

This bandana on my head does not mean
I do windows. I do knives, edge to head.
(I wear it around the house for days.
When the Avon lady came, she never
said a word, took my order. But never came back.)
Watch me slice air. Watch me
reweave it into a veil.

iv. What Hands May Do

Imitate peacocks.
Pray above the head.
Scoops bowls of air.
Place themselves.

Offer the shaking shoulders.
Stop everything but the hips.

       v. Ami Lesson

Think of it as rounding your equator.
Wherever your hips have traveled before
is nowhere compared to this. Reconnoiter four sites:
     front   circle side
     circle back   circle
     side   circle front.
Now, pilgrimage:
     Circle circle circle circle.
Let the trip by your hips', though your arms
may move air, confuse the currents of your torso,
your hot, happy torso. It may never come home.

HOLLY MITCHELL

SELF PORTRAIT WITH FRIED EGGS
Photograph by Sarah Lucas, 1996

I fry two hungers
over easy in the morning.
I put on these breasts,
drink coffee from styrofoam,

stare for strength.
This isn't a solicitation
for any working man to lick
the yolk from my t-shirt.

But if you do,
try.
Hands on the diner floor,
work up from my boots.

It's like I'm the heart
of Marlboro,
centerfold and selvage.
It's like I'm ordering

look when I fix you
this breakfast.
Should you objectify me—
please—leave the door open.

Julia Paganelli

ELEGY FOR THE WAITRESS'S BODY

I miscarry without telling anyone
    we have been fruitful.
Jackie still asks when that rickety husband and me
    will have one.
Asks how in our eagerness
    we haven't slipped yet.
I choke on the ridges of my hard laugh.
    Peach-stone under shallow ground.
Body is a bodice
    clutching my eyes.
It asks customers,
    How do you want your eggs?
On sizzling grill, Jackie cracks a bloody egg and jokes:
    Without rooster cum in them.
Spatula scrapes foamed yolk
    into disposal, white skinning.

Car hacks and spits behind the diner,
    the blank moon up.
Strange hands strip
    clothes from my rounded muscles.
I look up through the sun-roof,
    heat on HIGH,
hissing toward the eyes
    of driver and passenger seats.
Vents dry the skin of my shoulders,
    bare nipples pointed.
Trapped in cotton, he taps
    the car horn. Belts reel in the engine.

Cold edging into me,
    I feel no flaws in my form.

When he leaves me here, I am alone and I am naked,
    so I am supposed to be afraid.

SARAH FRELIGH

THE BIRTH MOTHER ON HER DAUGHTER'S FIRST BIRTHDAY

It's late and the woman one cell over
is finally quiet. Awake, she's at war
with life, *that motherfucker,* fights
sleep when it threatens to take her down
for the night, struggling
and punching the thin sheets
to keep what she imagines is hers.
The guard says it's snowing—
a real sonofabitch to drive in—
a foot already and more to fall.
On our first date, your father
drove to the KMart parking lot
and carved figure eights in the new snow.
I sat in the passenger's seat and said
go faster because I liked
how his biceps looked
under his flannel shirt
when he yanked that steering wheel
and made that car obey him.

I should tell you
everyone's innocent
in here. Guilt is a nametag we wear
for therapy sessions, tear up
and discard on the way out.
We sit in a circle and drink
bitter coffee, tell stories
that scald the tongue.
The day you were born you felt
like a bowl of hot pasta the doctor

spilled on my stomach. The nurse said
your baby is beautiful but she was wrong.
You looked like Eisenhower,
and you were never mine,
just something I might
have borrowed for a while.

KAREN L. GEORGE

THE SCREAM

Five days before you died,
when your pain spiked
and you could no longer swallow,
we agreed it was past time
for Hospice at home.

Waiting for the ambulance,
mind racing—
who to call,
words to tell them,
without you hearing,
keep myself halfway calm,
what to pack,
how many days,
you so quiet, distant,
thinking, feeling what—
I opened the door
to grab mail for the first time in days,
when a large spider crawled
over the threshold
as if invited to enter.

I doubled over, screamed
in its direction. Could almost see
my volume—the decibels—of my refusal,
the weight of those sound waves.

The spider vanished.
I searched the mottled door mat,
behind the stone wolf, geode, clay pot,
primed to stomp and smear.

When I told you why I yelled,
you winked, said you felt
a little sorry for the spider.

How amazing, to give
voice to all I'd held back.

HOPE JOHNSON

THE UNISEX SALON THAT GAVE ME BACK MY AFRO

She snips a *little papacito's,* first
calling him that, *little papacito.*

He sucks on a purple lollypop
licks hair from his fingers, some of it

falling between her breasts.
        His hair is straight as tailbone.

The other women chatter
and wait for my tongue's swing

from English, *just a hint*
or pennies from my afro

while Romeo and Marc make salsa
over the radio and the DJ shouts

to all my dominicanas, throw
your hands up and roll your hips mamis!

I keep my hands and hips to myself.
Yo también, yo también

The hairdresser throws up her arms
taps six inch heels

bare thighs slightly shimmy, open
her back laced in black mesh, curves

looking for *dominicana* in my afro.
Her breasts mimic air

around an hourglass. She flaunts
them, and tanned men, clean-cut

with god-like bodies, watch her hips
sway and scissors snip at my *cabesa,*

at the door, in the barber shop, between
Broadway, a converted closet and

Romeo Santos singing, *eres mia.*

ROGER BONAIR-AGARD

RETRIBUTION

after Jeff Donaldson's Wives of Shango *(1969)*

When the ghosts cross the oceans too, no telling
what they come to teach, to bring, to cause to shine.
Look—we black. Blistering in the sun, under guns
and look what God done give us to work from. They
say we come do the bidding of orishas an shit. I say
I'm bout to cap the first thing come for my man
and children. Sometimes, I massage gun oil
into my thighs from what's left over from the barrel—
orisha? Tell me who thunder and war then. Who
spirit done crossed this ocean, lay in these boats and wait
around long enough for this lash and water hose too.

This jaw got this set from sucking salt, from banding
my belly with these shells. I've lined my womb
with copper so I can turn these ash-filled churches
back to cities of light. You might think we separate
cross to bear, but we been Coptic to Nazareth and back
as one body; fingers itchy on a trigger and steadier
than a lead bannister. Nigga try me, see if this sister
don't duppy down on your head so hard you give
your land stakes back to a Blackfoot and ketch a slow
boat back. These rifles cuz we fed-up. These ghosts
cuz we tired and somebody gotta help us wth the carry.

We symmetry hands into angles of war
hip to elbow, bullet to jowl, see
how the light bless our cheekbones
like even God know apocalypse
and retribution the same song—black
and woman and all the tools to slit

a body clean from collar to groin
while humming the melodies at the heart
of all hymnals, at the skin of all drums

There is nothing like a woman
cross any border to see bout
her family. Guns and afros aint but a piece of the party.
we come in these colors of the sun and our brothers.
we hide under cover of broad
daylight. We carry blade and bible for what remains
when we raze
what's white
ghosts blaze, and barrel-spit—we fire
like what's bright. Bless the blood we shed—cross, ankh
or orisha, we verb black, action and still as stone.
only love fire point blank and dont blink
like this. We come and we come
back for our men, our children, our cities new
and full of light.

Shayla Lawson

LA MORETTA: (: : /)

I am also
called the servant
woman. Crazy,

how much I resemble
an absence.
The moon, new,

stripped off
its hinges,
dancing to light

in little girls :: gowns,
tinsel & I am tongue
tied—quite willing-

ly—ing \ grating
and capsizing
against my diffident up-

bringing. I take
my time
answering you in complete

silences. / / : these are
the marks where I bite
my tongue. Some say

I'm the great de-
fender. But I am not
just curves. I open

my lips and this mask
falls off. All I know to do
is survive.

NICKOLE BROWN

FUCK

is what she said, but what mattered was the tone—
not a drive-by spondee and never the fricative
connotation as verb, but from her mouth
voweled, often preceeded by *well*, with the "u" low
as if dipping up homemade ice cream, waiting to be served
last so that she'd scoop from the bottom
where all the good stuff had settled down.

Imagine: not a word cold-cocked or screwed to the wall
but something almost resigned, a sigh, an *oh, well*,
the f-word made so fat and slow it was basset hound,
chunky with an extra syllable, just enough weight
to make a jab to the ribs more of a shoulder shrug.
Think of what's done to "shit" in the South; this is
sheeee-aaatt but flicked with a whip, made a little more
tart. *Well, fuck, Betty Sue, I never did see that coming.*
Can you believe?

Or my favorite, not as explicative but noun—*fucker*,
she said, but what she meant was *darlin, sugar pie, sweet beets*,
a curse word made into a term of endearment, as in
Come here, you little fucker, and give your grandma a kiss.
If the child was young enough for diapers, he'd still be a *shitass*,
but big enough to lift his arms and touch his hands together
over his toddling tow head, he was *so big*, all grown, *a cute little*
fucker, watch him go.

Fuck is what she said, but what she needed was a drum,
a percussion to beat story into song, a chisel tapping
to crack the honey from the meanest rock,
not just *fuck if I know* or *fuck me running* or *fuck me*
sideways or *beats the fuck out of me* but said tender,

knowing there was only one thing in this whole world
you needed to hear most: *you fucker you, don't you know*
there wasn't a day when you weren't loved?

If you still don't understand, try this: a woman
up from poor soil, bad dirt, pure clay. A woman as
succulent, something used to precious little
water, hard sun. Rock crop maybe, threading roots
able to suck nutrients from the nothing
of gravel, the nothing of stone, a thriving thing
sturdy, thorned, green out of mere
spite, and because you least expect it,
laughing, cussing up a storm—my grandmother
who didn't ask for power but took it
in bright, full, fuck-it-all bloom.

KATE HADFIELD

ON MY KNEES

if I have lost you
so that I could find him—
sisters, forgive me.

if I have closed myself to your arms
with a dream of his—
sisters, forgive me.

I am petrified.
stuck with my arms
stretching to his house,
moss has grown on my fingertips,
covered my eyebrows.
birds have become my hair.
their little feet found homes in my head.
the grass sprouted thick thigh-high,
and my eyes have closed
to everything but his front door.
sisters,
forgive me.

Grandmother,
reach for my hands.
I have forgotten my mouth.
it got lost in the flood.
teach me again how to speak.

Mother,
I have dismissed your prayers,
I thought my own wisdom was enough.
have mercy on me.

I have burned myself at the stake.
thrown myself into the river,
hands bound.
I cannot find my voice.
I cannot find my feet.
women,
bathe me.
show me my toes like a newborn,
we can pretend it's the first time
I've seen them.

sisters,
I have forgotten my sex.
I have forgotten humility.

Gaea, forgive me,
I forgot reverence.

Isis, forgive me,
I lost strength.
Hera,

I forgot anger—
Aphrodite,
I indulged lust-
forgive me.

Lucille Clifton,
please forgive me,
I forgot my hips.
Anne Sexton,

I ignored my art.
Dorothy Parker,
I forgot my mind.
Emily Dickinson,
you must forgive me,
I dismissed my own body.
I could not see the flowers.

Sharon Olds,
Shekina,
Gloria Steinem
look at me.
Mary Magdalene,
Alice Walker,
Oshun,
hear me.
Eve,
Kwan Yin,
Yemanja,
White Buffalo Woman,
forgive me.
forgive,
I beg you.
Great Mother,
bless me again.

I have been petrified
with my arms reaching towards him.
women,
come to me.
I know I have forsaken you,

but reach for me,
show me
you are still there.
I know.

SHARON L. CHARDE

HUNGRY

I'm the most beautiful woman in the world. I can get
the ring to go back in the bell, the rose to return

to the bud, the wrinkled skin to smooth out. I am holy
mary mother of god, I wash your moment clean of need

and grasp. I can do anything you want, get you to tap,
paint your face with glitter whorls, blow up balloons

for the party of us. I'm a rock concert, I play so loud
you have to hear me. Listen. I'm extravagant, your girl

in a string bikini that can fit into a thimble, an adventure
you're dying to have, your lucky charm. I'm a sorcerer,

spinning god around like a hula hoop, crazed by the piece
of moon you left. Wait, don't leave the party yet, I have

more tricks, music, a fat cigar, a bottle of good champagne,
a feather boa. Don't squander my dazzling notes. Stay,

make another soundtrack with me, kill the echo of that old
adagio, ripe and burning.

BIANCA LYNNE SPRIGGS

WHAT WOMEN ARE MADE OF

> There are many kinds of open
>
> —Audre Lorde, *Coal*

We are all ventricle, spine, lung, larynx, and gut.
Clavicle and nape, what lies forked in an open palm;

we are follicle and temple. We are ankle, arch,
sole. Pore and rib, pelvis and root,

and tongue. We are wishbone and gland and molar
and lobe. We are hippocampus and exposed nerve

and cornea. Areola, pigment, melanin, and nails.
Varicose. Cellulite. Divining rod. Sinew and tissue,

saliva and silt. We are blood and salt, clay and aquifer.
We are breath and flame and stratosphere. Palimpsest

and bibelot and cloisonné fine lines. Marigold, hydrangea,
and dimple. Nightlight, satellite, and stubble. We are

pinnacle, plummet, dark circles and dark matter.
A constellation of freckles and specters and miracles

and lashes. Both bent and erect, we are all give
and give back. We are volta and girder. Make an incision

in our nectary and Painted Ladies sail forth, riding the back
of a warm wind, plumed with love and things like love.

Crack us down to the marrow, and you may find us full
of cicada husks and sand dollars and salted maple taffy

weary of welding together our daydreams. All sweet tea,
razor blades, carbon, and patchwork quilts of *Good God!*

and *Lord Have Mercy!* Our hands remember how to turn
the earth before we do. Our intestinal fortitude? Cumulonimbus

streaked with saffron light. Our foundation? Not in our limbs
or hips; this comes first as an amen, a hallelujah, a suckling,

swaddled psalm sung at the cosmos' breast. You want to
know what women are made of? Open wide and find out.

ABOUT THE AUTHORS

tina andry is a writer. she is the author of the chapbook *ransom notes*. she has two children. she is a coffee snob.

Britt Ashley is a queer femme from Texas currently living in Portland, Oregon with her handsome husbian and their small animal circus. Her poetry and artwork has appeared or is forthcoming in *The Offing, juked, Winter Tangerine Review, cream city review,* and elsewhere.

Stacey Balkun, author of *Lost City Museum* (ELJ Publications, 2016) received her MFA from Fresno State and her work has appeared or will appear in *Ekphrasis, Gargoyle, Muzzle, THRUSH, Bodega,* and others. Stacey has been a 2015 Hambidge Fellow and a 2013 Artist-in-Residence at the Great Smoky Mountains National Park.

Makalani Bandele is an Affrilachian Poet and Louisville, Kentucky native. He is the recipient of fellowships from Millay Colony, Vermont Studio Center, Kentucky Arts Council, and Cave Canem Foundation. His poems can be read in various online and print journals. *Hellfightin',* published by Willow Books is his first full-length volume of poetry.

Bianca Bargo is a Kentucky woman, a transplant to Lexington from the eastern coalfields. Winner of the UK Farquhar Poetry Award in 2009, her work has been published in the University of Kentucky's literary journal *Limestone,* as well as Accent Publishing's *Bigger Than They Appear: An Anthology of Very Short Poems.* Her debut chapbook, *How I Became an Angry Woman,* is now available from Accents Publishing.

Ellen Bass's poetry includes *Like a Beggar, The Human Line,* and *Mules of Love,* and she co-edited the groundbreaking anthology, *No More Masks!* Her work has frequently appeared in *The New Yorker, The American Poetry Review,* and many other journals. She teaches in the MFA program at Pacific University. *www.ellenbass.com.*

Roberta Beary, an editor at *Modern Haiku,* tweets her photoku *@shortpoemz.* Her book *The Unworn Necklace* is a William Carlos Williams award finalist (Poetry Society of America). Her most recent book is *Deflection.* She travels worldwide to give readings and workshops on the art of the short poem.

Elizabeth Beck is a teacher, writer and artist who lives with her family on a pond in Lexington, Kentucky. She is the author of two books of poetry.

In 2011, she founded The Teen Howl Poetry Series that serves the youth of central Kentucky.

Lauren Boisvert is a creative writing major at the University of Central Florida. She has had poems published in journals such as *Mochila Review, Young Writers Anthology, The Broken Plate*, and others. She was recently chosen as runner up in The Poet's Billow 2015 Pangaea Prize for poetry, and one time she walked really close to David Sedaris while he was signing books.

Roger Bonair-Agard wrote *Bury My Clothes*. The National Book Awards long listed it. The Society for Midland Authors gave it its Poetry Award. He's from Trinidad. He's from Brooklyn. He founded and facilitates The Baldwin Protocols: an arts based intervention for students of color in higher learning. He is the Director of Creative Writing at Free Write Arts & Literacy. He lives in Chicago.

Nickole Brown's first collection, *Sister,* was published by Red Hen Press, and *Fanny Says* came out from BOA Editions in 2015. Currently, she is the Editor for the Marie Alexander Series in Prose Poetry and is on faculty at the Writing Workshops in Greece and the low-residency MFA Program in Creative Writing at Murray State.

Elizabeth Burton is a senior English student at Transylvania University. Her work has been featured in the *Albion Review,* the 2014 and 2015 Lexington Poetry Month anthologies, as well as *PublishED,* the University of Edinburgh's literary magazine. When she isn't writing poems about ghosts, she is probably napping.

Gregory L Candela is a professor emeritus at University of New Mexico and has resided in New Mexico since 1972. He holds a doctorate in American literature from UNM and is author of six produced plays. Recent publications include poems in *Malpaís Review, Adobe Walls, Monterey Bay Review* and *Italian Americana.*

Poet and paper artist, **Terry Ann Carter**, is the author of five collections of lyric poetry and five chapbooks of haiku. She is an instructor of Japanese literary forms at Royal Roads University, Victoria, British Columbia and president of Haiku Canada.

Linda Casebeer lives in Birmingham, Alabama. She has published *The Last Eclipsed Moon,* from Cherry Grove Collections, and poems in *Slant, Earth's Daughters, Chest,* and *Hospital Drive, Knowing Stones* and *The Light in Ordinary Things* among others. She and her husband have recently published a novel, *The Canary Room.*

Sherry Chandler is the author of four poetry collections, most recently *The Woodcarver's Wife* (Wind Publications). Her work has appeared in such journals as *The Cortland Review, The South Carolina Review, The Louisville Review, Kestrel* and *The Blue Fifth Review.*

Sharon Charde, retired psychotherapist, writing workshop facilitator for women and delinquent girls since 1990, is an award-winning poet with six published collections, one of which was dramatized as a radio play for the BBC broadcast in June 2012. She has seven Pushcart nominations, many fellowships and wide journal publication.

Lucia Cherciu is a Professor of English at SUNY / Dutchess Community College in Poughkeepsie, New York and her latest book of poetry is *Edible Flowers* (Main Street Rag, 2015). Her poetry has been nominated for a Pushcart Prize and for Best of the Net. *luciacherciu.webs.com.*

Elizabeth Cohen is a professor of English at SUNY Plattsburgh and the co-editor of *Saranac Review.* She is the author of a memoir, *The House on Beartown Road,* a book of short stories, *The Hypothetical Girl,* and four books of poetry.

Star Coulbrooke, Poet Laureate of Logan City Utah, is responsible for Helicon West, a bi-monthly open readings/featured readers series. Her poems appear in journals such as *Poetry International, Soundings East,* and *Sugar House Review.* Star directs the Utah State University Writing Center.

Barbara Crooker's poems have appeared in journals and anthologies including *The Bedford Introduction to Literature* and *Good Poems American Places.* She has six full-length books of poetry, including *Small Rain* (Purple Flag Press, 2014) and *Barbara Crooker: Selected Poems* (FutureCycle Press, 2015).

Lucille Lang Day (*lucillelangday.com*) is the author of ten poetry collections and chapbooks, including *Becoming an Ancestor* and *Dreaming of Sunflowers: Museum Poems,* which received the 2014 Blue Light Poetry

Prize. Her poems, stories and essays have appeared widely in magazines and anthologies; her award-winning memoir is *Married at Fourteen.*

Nancy Diedrichs is the creative director and broadcast producer at a local ad agency and former front-lady of a rock band. She's an avid gardener of tomatoes, an ungraceful but enthusiastic dancer, a lover of animals and wife to singer-songwriter Eric, one of the most compassionate guys on the planet.

Joanie DiMartino is the author of two collections of poetry. She is currently finishing her third manuscript, *Wood to Skin,* about the 19th-century whaling industry, which inspired a sequence of "Sally Brown" poems. DiMartino directs the Hidden Treasures Poetry Series in downtown Mystic, Connecticut. She has a background in suffrage history and works in historic house museums.

Laurel Dixon lives in Lexington, Kentucky. She won first place in The Carnegie Center's LGBT Writing Contest for her story *How to Fall in Love with Straight Girls,* and her poetry has been published in *Tobacco Magazine, Words Dance Magazine, Pollen* and *The Legendary.* She spends most of her time writing, gardening, and drinking too much coffee.

Teneice Durrant is the Managing Editor of Argus House Press and the co-editor of *Small Batch,* a collection of bourbon poetry, from Two of Cups Press.

Meg Eden's work has been published in various magazines, including *Rattle, Drunken Boat, Poet Lore,* and *Gargoyle.* She teaches at the University of Maryland. She has four poetry chapbooks, and her novel *Post-High School Reality Quest* is forthcoming from California Coldblood, an imprint of Rare Bird Lit. Check out her work at: *www.megedenbooks.com.*

Lynnell Edwards is the author of three full length collections of poetry, most recently *Covet* (Red Hen Press, 2011) and a chapbook *Kings of the Rock and Roll Hot Shop* (Accents publishing, 2014). She is associate professor of English at Spalding University.

Marta Ferguson is the co-editor of *Drawn to Marvel: Poems from the Comic Books* (Minor Arcana Press, 2014) and the author of *Mustang Sally Pays Her Debt to Wilson Pickett* (Main Street Rag, 2005). She is the sole proprietor of Wordhound Writing & Editing Services, LLC (*www.wordhound.com*).

Ruth Foley lives in Massachusetts, where she teaches English for Wheaton College. Her work appears in numerous web and print journals, including *Antiphon, The Bellingham Review,* and *Sou'wester.* She is the author of two chapbooks, *Dear Turquoise* (dancing girl press) and *Creature Feature* (ELJ Publications), and serves as Managing Editor for *Cider Press Review.*

Sarah Freligh is the author of *Sad Math,* winner of the 2014 Moon City Poetry Prize, *Sort of Gone,* and *A Brief Natural History of An American Girl.* Among her awards are a 2009 poetry fellowship from the National Endowment for the Arts and a poetry grant from the Constance Saltonstall Foundation in 2006.

Karen George, author of *Into the Heartland, Inner Passage, Swim Your Way Back, Seed of Me,* and forthcoming *The Fire Circle,* has work in *Memoir, Louisville Review, Naugatuck River Review,* and *Still.* She reviews poetry at *readwritepoetry.blogspot.com,* and is fiction editor of the journal *Waypoints.* Visit her website at: *karenlgeorge.snack.ws.*

Kate Hadfield is a writer, dancer, and choreographer currently living in Lexington, Kentucky. Hadfield's life work is storytelling, more specifically telling the stories of women. Both real and fantastical, from Rapunzel to her own mother, Kate believes all women are connected, all sisters, all ancestors and descendants.

Ellen Hagan is the author of *Hemisphere,* Northwestern University Press, 2015 & *Crowned,* Sawyer House Press, 2010. She is the director of the poetry program at the DreamYard Project in New York City, and recently joined the visiting faculty in West Virginia Wesleyan's low residency MFA program.

Gwen Hart teaches writing at Buena Vista University in Storm Lake, Iowa. Her second poetry collection, *The Empress of Kisses,* won the 2015 X.J. Kennedy Prize from Texas Review Press and will be published in 2016. Her previous book, *Lost and Found* (David Robert Books), is available on Amazon.

Lisa Hartz lives in the Tidewater region of Virginia with her husband and four sons. "Incantation, Translation," originally published in *Redivider* as "Portrait of the Herbalist, Doris Ulmann, 1929," is drawn from a manuscript exploring the life and work of photographer Doris Ulmann.

Sheryl Morang Holmberg is a poet and writer living in Michigan. Her work has been published in journals such as the *Driftwood Review, Earth's Daughters, Washington Square, Cumberland Poetry Review,* and *Edgz.* Sheryl has taught poetry and creative writing as a visiting writer in Detroit Public Schools. She currently works as a freelance writer and editor.

Karen Paul Holmes is the author of the poetry collection, *Untying the Knot* (Aldrich Press, 2014). Publishing credits include *Poetry East, Atlanta Review, Atticus Review, The Sow's Ear Poetry Review, Kentucky Review, Lascaux Review, Southern Poetry Anthology Vol 5: Georgia* (Texas Review Press) and many more.

Hope Johnson is Education Program Coordinator of Brooklyn Public Library's Read! Write! Create! Literacy Program for struggling readers in NYC Housing Authority communities. Hope received her MFA in Creative Writing from Lesley University and is a 2014 Pushcart Prize Nominee. Her recent publications are found in *Loose Change* and *Valley Voices.*

Julia Johnson is the author of *Naming the Afternoon* and *The Falling Horse.* Her most recent poetry collection, *Subsidence,* is forthcoming in 2016. Her poems have appeared in *The Cincinnati Review, Poetry International, The Greensboro Review, Sentence: A Journal of Prose Poetics, Washington Square,* and numerous other journals and anthologies. She directs the MFA Program at the University of Kentucky.

Susan Johnson has her MFA and PhD from the University of Massachusetts Amherst where she teaches writing in the Isenberg School of Management. Her poems have recently appeared in *Rhino, Freshwater, Comstock Review, Oyez Review, Pinyon, THEODATE, Bluestem,* and *Karamu.* Her chapbook *Impossible is Nothing* was published by Finishing Line Press.

Amanda Johnston earned her MFA in Creative Writing from Stonecoast at the University of Southern Maine. She is a member of the Affrilachian Poets, a Cave Canem graduate fellow, and is the founder and executive director of Torch Literary Arts. Visit her website at *www.amandajohnston.com.*

Marilyn Kallet is the author of 17 books including *The Love That Moves Me,* poetry by Black Widow Press. She has translated Paul Eluard, Benjamin

Péret, and Chantal Bizzini. Dr. Kallet is Nancy Moore Goslee Professor of English at the University of Tennessee, and she leads poetry workshops for VCCA in Auvillar, France.

A prize-winning poet, **Penelope Karageorge** is the author of two novels and two poetry collections, *Red Lipstick and the Wine-Dark Sea* (Pella) and *The Neon Suitcase* (Somerset Hall Press). She is now planning production of a film, *Drinking the Sun,* a romantic comedy set on the Greek island of Lemnos.

Diane Kendig—poet, writer, translator and teacher for 40 years—has authored four poetry collections, most recently *The Places We Find Ourselves.* A recipient of two Ohio Arts Council Fellowships, she has poems recently in *J Journal, Wordgathering,* and *Ekphrasis,* among others. She's on the web: *dianekendig.com* and *dianekendig.blogspot.com.*

Karen Kovacik is the author of *Beyond the Velvet Curtain* and *Metropolis Burning.* Her poems and translations of contemporary Polish poetry have appeared in numerous journals, including *APR, Boston Review, Southern Review* and *West Branch.* In 2016, her anthology of contemporary Polish women poets, *Scattering the Dark,* will appear from White Pine Press.

Shayla Lawson is a professional educator, recreational acrobat, and a member of the Affrilachian Poets. Her work has appeared in *Guernica, The Journal, Colorado Review,* and *MiPOesias.* Her work is supported by fellowships provided through the Kentucky Foundation for Women, Indiana University, the Giorgio Cini Foundation, and Kentucky Governor's School for the Arts.

Emily Leider has published four biographies and one poetry collection, *Rapid Eye Movement.* Her poems have appeared in *December Magazine, Caveat Lector, The Chicago Review* and other periodicals. Her short story "Twins" ran recently in *Open Road Review.* A native New Yorker, she lives in San Francisco.

Marsha Mathews is a Professor of English at Dalton State College. Her first chapbook, *Northbound Single-Lane* was published in 2010 by Finishing Line Press. Her second, *Sunglow & a Tuft of Nottingham Lace,* won the 2011 chapbook competition at Redberry Editions. Marsha's most recent book is *Hallelujah Voices,* Aldrich Press, 2012.

Andrew Merton's first book of poetry, *Evidence that We Are Descended from Chairs* (Accents Publishing, 2012) was named Outstanding Book of Poetry, 2013–2014, by the new Hampshire Writers' Project. Accents Publishing released his second book, *Lost and Found*, in 2015. He is a professor emeritus of English at the University of New Hampshire.

Teresa Milbrodt has published a short story collection, *Bearded Women: Stories;* a novel, *The Patron Saint of Unattractive People;* and a flash fiction collection, *Larissa Takes Flight: Stories.* Her stories, poems, and flash fiction have appeared in numerous literary magazines, and her work has been nominated for a Pushcart Prize.

Pamela Miller's wild woman credentials include being published in the anthologies *Dangerous Dames* and *Daughter of Dangerous Dames* back in the 1990s. Her latest collection of poetry is *Miss Unthinkable* (Mayapple Press, 2013). She lives in Chicago with her husband, science fiction writer Richard Chwedyk, who's pretty wild himself.

Holly Mitchell is an MFA candidate at New York University. Her poems have appeared or are forthcoming in several journals including *Washington Square, Ishaan Literary Review, Split Quarterly, The Bakery,* and *Transom.* In 2012, she received a Gertrude Claytor Prize from Mount Holyoke College and the Academy of American Poets.

Sarah Fawn Montgomery is the author of *The Astronaut Checks His Watch* (Finishing Line Press). Her poetry and prose have appeared in various magazines including *Confrontation, Crab Orchard Review, DIAGRAM, Fugue, Georgetown Review, The Los Angeles Review, North Dakota Quarterly, The Pinch, Puerto del Sol, Southeast Review, Zone 3* and others.

Translator and poet **Maria Nazos** is the author of *A Hymn That Meanders,* (2011, Wising Up Press). Her work is published or forthcoming in *The North American Review, The Florida Review, The Southern Humanities Review, The New Ohio Review,* and elsewhere. She can be found at *www.marianazos.com.*

Sheryl L. Nelms is from Marysville, Kansas. She graduated from South Dakota State University. She has had over 5,000 articles, stories and poems published, including fourteen individual collections of her poems. She is a three time Pushcart Prize nominee.

Jeremy Paden is a member of the Affrilachian Poets and an Associate Professor of Spanish and Latin American literature at Transylvania University. He is the author of the chapbook *Broken Tulips* (Accents Publishing, 2013). His poems have appeared in *Beloit Poetry Journal, Cortland Review, Louisville Review, pluck!, Rattle* and other places.

Julia Paganelli is an MFA candidate in her second year at the University of Arkansas. Her chapbook, *Blush Less,* was released through Finishing Line Press in February 2015. She has also been published by *BOAAT, Chautauqua Literary Journal, Hobart,* and *The Madison Review,* among others.

Tina Parker lives in Berea, Kentucky, with her husband and two young daughters. Her full-length poetry collection *Mother May I* will be published by Sibling Rivalry Press in 2016. Individual poems have appeared in *Rattle, PMS: poemmemoirstory,* and *The Collapsar,* among others. To learn more about Tina, visit *www.tina-parker.com.*

Catherine Perkins, survivor, mother, equestrian, farmer and poet, started writing as a teen. She recently reunited with pen and paper, after becoming semi-retired. Her goals as a writer are to be highly regarded and often read. Her goals as a human—make people laugh, regard everyone highly and become well read.

Kiki Petrosino is the author of two books of poetry: *Hymn for the Black Terrific* (2013) and *Fort Red Border* (2009), both from Sarabande Books. She is an Associate Professor of English at the University of Louisville, where she directs the Creative Writing Program.

Sosha Pinson is originally from Pikeville, Kentucky. She received her MFA in Poetry from Drew University's Low Residency Program and her BFA in Creative Writing from Morehead State University. Her recent poems can be seen or are forthcoming in *The Wide Shore, Minerva Rising, Still: The Journal,* among others.

Carol Quinn's poetry has appeared in *32 Poems, The Cincinnati Review, Colorado Review, Pleiades,* and other journals. *Acetylene,* her first book of poems, was selected by Dorothy Barresi for the 2008 Cider Press Review Book Award and published in 2010. Quinn also recently won the So to Speak Poetry Prize.

Hila Ratzabi was selected by Adrienne Rich for a National Writers Union Poetry Prize. Her poetry has been published in *Narrative, Alaska Quarterly Review, Drunken Boat, Linebreak, The Nervous Breakdown,* and others. She holds an MFA from Sarah Lawrence, is editor-in-chief of *Storyscape,* and lives in Philadelphia.

Nicholas Samaras is the author of *Hands of the Saddlemaker* (Yale University Press), and *American Psalm, World Psalm* (Ashland Poetry Press). Other work has appeared in *The New Yorker, Poetry, Image, Kenyon Review,* and elsewhere. He is currently completing a new manuscript of poetry, and serves as the Poetry Editor of *The Adirondack Review.*

Leona Sevick's work appears in *The Journal, Barrow Street, Potomac Review* and other journals. She is the 2012 first place winner of the *Split This Rock* Poetry contest, judged by Naomi Shihab Nye. Her first chapbook, *Damaged Little Creatures,* was published in 2015 by FutureCycle Press (*www.leonasevick.com*). She is associate provost and associate professor of English at Mount St. Mary's University.

Not only a poet, **Hilary Sheers** is a commercial translator and editor and visual artist. Currently revising and editing the English translation of a new collection by Ukrainian poet and Pen award winner, Ihor Pavyluk, for US publication. She has a degree in Philosophy and spent 20 years as an adult education lecturer.

Dan Sicoli released two poetry chapbooks through Pudding House Publications: *Pagan Supper* and *the allegories.* Recent work has appeared in *Chiron Review, Bop Dead City, Red Paint Hill Poetry Journal, Santa Fe Literary Review, EXPERIMEMENTOS, Architrave, Up the Staircase,* and *Nerve Cowboy.* He co-edits *Slipstream* (*www.slipstreampress.org*) in Niagara Falls, NY.

Founding editor of *Pearl* and *Bukowski Review,* UCIrvine MFA grad, Pushcart honoree, Forward Prize Finalist, **Joan Jobe Smith** has appeared internationally in 1000+ publications, including 22 poetry collections, and two prose memoirs: *Charles Bukowski: EPIC GLOTTIS: His Art & His Women (& me)* and *Tales of An Ancient Go-Go Girl.*

Bianca Lynne Spriggs is an Affrilachian Poet and Cave Canem Fellow. She is the author of *Kaffir Lily* (Wind Publications), *How Swallowtails Become Dragons* (Accents Publishing), and the forthcoming collections, *Call Her*

By Her Name (Northwestern University Press), and the *Galaxy is a Dance Floor* (Argos Books). She is the Managing Editor for *pluck! The Journal of Affrilachian Arts & Culture* and Poetry Editor for *Apex Magazine.*

Alison Stone wrote *Dangerous Enough, Borrowed Logic, From the Fool to the World,* and *They Sing at Midnight,* which won the 2003 Many Mountains Moving Award. She was awarded Poetry's Frederick Bock Prize and New York Quarterly's Madeline Sadin award. She created The Stone Tarot and is a psychotherapist.

Katerina Stoykova-Klemer is the author of several poetry books in English and Bulgarian, most recently *The Porcupine of Mind* (Broadstone Books, English) and *How God Punishes* (ICU, Bulgarian), which won the Ivan Nikolov National Poetry Prize. Katerina co-wrote the independent feature film *Proud Citizen,* directed by Thom Southerland, and acted in the lead role.

Victoria Sullivan is a Master's student of English Literature at the University of Kentucky, particularly interested in Appalachian literature and its social and cultural implications. Her work can be found in *The Quaker* (Malone University), *Still: The Journal,* and *This Wretched Vessel,* the 2014 Lexington Poetry Month publication.

Mariahadessa Ekere Tallie is the author of *Dear Continuum: Letters to a Poet Crafting Liberation* (Grand Concourse Press) and *Karma's Footsteps* (Flipped Eye). She is the Poetry Editor of the literary magazine *African Voices.* Tallie's work is the subject of the short film *I Leave My Colors Everywhere.*

A native of Memphis, **Sheree Renée Thomas**'s work has been previously published or is forthcoming in *Callaloo, storySouth, Eleven Eleven, Mythic Delirium, Transition,* and in the anthologies *An Alphabet of Embers, Stories for Chip: A Tribute to Samuel R. Delany, Memphis Noir, The Moment of Change* edited by Rose Lemberg, *The Ringing Ear* edited by Nikky Finney, and others. Visit *shereereneethomas.wordpress.com.*

Jessica D. Thompson's work appears in journals such as *Atlanta Review* and *The Sow's Ear,* and in the anthology *New Poetry from the Midwest* (New American Press). She is the recipient of the 2013 James Baker Hall Memorial Prize in Poetry (New Southerner), the Kudzu Poetry Prize

(2014), and is the author of a poetry chapbook entitled *Bullets and Blank Bibles* (Liquid Paper Press).

Alison Townsend is the author of two poetry collections, *Persephone in America* and *The Blue Dress*. Her poetry appears widely and she has won a Pushcart Prize and appeared in *The Best American Poetry*. Emerita Professor of English at the University of Wisconsin-Whitewater, she is completing an essay collection, *The Name for Woman is River: Remembering the Landscapes of Home*.

Rosemerry Wahtola Trommer's poetry has appeared in *O Magazine*, in *back alleys*, on *A Prairie Home Companion* and on *river rocks*. She was recently appointed Poet Laureate of Colorado's Western Slope. Since 2005, she's written a poem a day. Favorite one-word mantra: Adjust.

A literary activist, **Elsa Valmidiano**'s works appear in numerous literary journals and anthologies. She is also Fiction Editor of *As/Us,* a journal publishing works by underrepresented women writers. Elsa holds an MFA from Mills College, is a member of the Philippine American Writers and Artists, Inc., and resides in Oakland with her husband. Find her on Twitter *@Evalmidiano*.

Multidisciplinary artist and Danville, Kentucky native, **Frank X Walker**, is the former Poet Laureate of Kentucky, co-founder of the Affrilachian Poets, and the author of seven collections of poetry including *Turn Me Loose: The Unghosting of Medgar Evers,* winner of the 2014 NAACP Image Award for best poetry collection, and *About Flight*.

Amy Watkins is a poet, visual artist, and teacher who lives in Orlando, Florida, with her husband and daughter. Her chapbook *Milk & Water* is available from Yellow Flag Press.

Patricia Wellingham-Jones is a widely published former psychology researcher and writer/editor. She has a special interest in healing writing, with poems recently in *The Widow's Handbook* (Kent State University Press). Chapbooks include *Don't Turn Away: poems about breast cancer, End-Cycle: poems about caregiving, Apple Blossoms at Eye Level, Hormone Stew*.

July Westhale is a poet and essayist living in Oakland, California. She is the author of *The Cavalcade,* forthcoming from Finishing Line Press in 2016, and has been awarded grants and residencies from the Vermont

Studio Center, the Lambda Literary Foundation, Sewanee, Tomales Bay, Dickinson House, Tin House and Bread Loaf. *www.julywesthale.com*.

K. Nicole Wilson lives and writes in Lexington, Kentucky, where she's just a hop and skip from her family, and hometown, Maysville. Her words appear in various journals and she often reads at local open mics. The University of Kentucky and Spalding should both be proud to call her an alumnus.

Laura Madeline Wiseman is the author of over twenty books and chapbooks and the editor of *Women Write Resistance: Poets Resist Gender Violence* (Hyacinth Girl Press, 2013). Her most recent book is *Drink* (BlazeVOX Books, 2015). She teaches at the University of Nebraska-Lincoln. *www.lauramadelinewiseman.com*.

Jessica Wright is a graduate student in Classics. She also teaches literature and Latin in local prisons. Her poetry has appeared in various venues, most recently *Tellus* (2015) and the Lines + Stars Broadside Project in Washington, DC (fall 2015).

Debra Woolley is an assistant professor of English at Broward College in Davie, Florida. She is originally from Jamaica and now lives in Fort Lauderdale, Florida with her husband, Jeffrey, and son, Jackson. She likes watching movies, gardening, and playing with her son.

Katy Yocom's fiction, poetry, and essays have appeared in *The Louisville Review, New Southerner, Open 24 Hrs, Louisville Magazine,* and *LEO Weekly*. Her journalism has appeared in *The Boston Globe, The San Diego Union-Tribune,* and elsewhere. She is a graduate of the Spalding University low-residency MFA in Writing program.

ACKNOWLEDGMENTS

"Film Adaptation of a Love Scene from My Unread Copy of *Wuthering Heights*" by Britt Ashley was previously published in *juked* in February 2015.

"Lilith" by Stacey Balkun was previously published in *The Saranac Review,* Issue 10, 2014, page 173.

"I Don't Know Why I Sucked Your Dick" and "Ophelia" by Bianca Bargo were previously published in *How I Became an Angry Woman* (Accents Publishing, 2015).

Ellen Bass, "How I Became Miss America" from *Like a Beggar*. Copyright © 2014 by Ellen Bass. "In Praise of Four-letter Words" from *The Human Line*. Copyright © 2007 by Ellen Bass. Reprinted with the permission of The Permissions Company, Inc. on behalf of Copper Canyon Press, *www.coppercanyonpress.org*.

"Afterglow" by Roberta Beary was previously published in *Deflection* (Accents Publishing, 2015).

Nickole Brown, "Fuck" from *Fanny Says*. Originally published in *Oxford American* #81 (Summer 2013). Copyright © 2013, 2015 by Nickole Brown. Reprinted with the permission of The Permissions Company, Inc., on behalf of BOA Editions, Ltd., *www.boaeditions.org*.

"Hungry" by Sharon L. Charde was previously published in *After Blue* (Finishing Line Press, 2014).

"Shopper" by Star Coulbrooke was published with a different title and in a slightly different form in *Logan Canyon Blend,* Blue Scarab Press, Pocatello, Idaho, 2003.

"Cactus Club Dancer, Afternoon Shift," by Star Coulbrooke was published in *15 Bytes,* Utah's Art Magazine, "Sunday Blog Read," August 3, 2014.

"Janis" by Barbara Crooker was previously published in *Texas Poetry Review*.

"Snow White Turns Sixty" by Barbara Crooker was previously published in *Ardent*.

"Delinquent Sonnets" and "Angenette Sampson" by Lucille Lang Day were previously published in *Becoming an Ancestor: Poems* (Červená Barva Press, 2015).

"Solace" by Teneice Durrant was previously published in *Burden of Solace* (Červená Barva Press, 2012).

"Another Woman" by Teneice Durrant was previously published in *The Goldilocks Complex* (Rocksaw Press, 2009).

"Suite For Wives" from *The Highwayman's Wife* by Lynnell Edwards. Copyright 2007 by Lynnell Edwards. Red Hen Press: Pasadena. Reprinted with permission by Red Hen Press. All Rights Reserved.

"Easy" and "The Birth Mother on Her Daughter's First Birthday" by Sarah Freligh were previously published in *A Brief Natural History of an American Girl* (Accents Publishing, 2011).

"The Scream" by Karen L. George was previously published in *Swim Your Way Back* (Dos Madres Press, 2014).

"Paean: Man in the Moon" by Gregory L. Candela was previously published in *Harwood Anthology,* Harwood Art Center, Old School Books, Albuquerque, NM, 2006, p. 40.

"Galatea Alone" by Gwen Hart was previously published in *Measure: A Review of Formal Poetry* 3.1 (Fall 2008).

"Incantation, Translation Portrait of the Herbalist, Doris Ulmann, Lang Syne Plantation, South Carolina, Circa 1929–1921" by Lisa Hartz was previously published in the Fall 2015 Issue of *Redivider* as "Portrait of the Herbalist, Lang Syne Plantation, Doris Ulmann, 1929."

"Anima Mundi" by Sheryl Holmberg was previously published under the title "Sestina for a Snake" in *Cumberland Poetry Review,* Fall 1997.

"The Woman in the City" by Julia Johnson was previously published in *The Falling Horse* (Factory Hollow Press, 2012) under the title "Woman in the Intricate City."

"It Ain't Prostitution" by Amanda Johnston was previously published in her chapbook *Guap.*

"Circe, After Hours" by Marilyn Kallet was previously published in *Circe, After Hours*, BkMk Press, 2005; reprinted in *Packing Light: New and Selected Poems*, Black Widow Press, 2009.

"Basha Teaching Balady" by Diane Kendig was previously published in *Middle Eastern Dancer*. ©1991 Diane Kendig.

"Frida Kahlo's Self-Portrait with Monkey" by Diane Kendig was previously published in *Solo Flyer*. ©1997 Diane Kendig.

"To My Last Period" by Karen Kovacik was previously published in *Atticus Review*.

"The Ticket for Wives at the Annual Woodworking Show" by Meg Eden was previously published in *Words Dance*.

"La Moretta: (: : /)" by Shayla Lawson was previously published in *The Journal*.

"The Woman Who Wasn't His Wife" by Marsha Mathews was previously published in *Hallelujah Voices* (Aldrich Press, 2012).

"Cruise Ship Intervention" by Andrew Merton was previously published in *Evidence that We Are Descended from Chairs* (Accents Publishing, 2012).

"Stop" by Tina Parker was previously published in *The Collapsar*, January 2014.

"Soliloquies at the Outer Banks" by Carol Quinn was previously published in *Acetylene* (Cider Press Review, 2010).

"Sedna the Arctic Sea Goddess" by Hila Ratzabi was previously published in *Alaska Quarterly Review*.

"Eve Naming Other Animals" by Nicholas Samaras was previously published in *New England Review*, Volume 16, Number 3. Vermont: Middlebury College (Summer, 1994): 115-116.

"Statement" by Hilary Sheers was previously published in *Uncertain Age* (Manifold, 2000).

"Out of Sight" by Joan Jobe Smith was previously published in *Chiron Review* in 1988.

"Persephone Returning" by Alison Stone was previously published in *Poetry* (Chicago) and *They Sing at Midnight* (Many Mountains Moving Press, 2003).

"One Should Exercise Caution" by Katerina Stoykova-Klemer was previously published in *The Porcupine of Mind* (Broadstone Books, 2012).

"Diana" by Jessica D. Thompson was previously published in *Appalachian Heritage Magazine*.

"You Hit Like a Girl" and "Time Is Thinner Than Glass" by Frank X Walker were previously published in *About Flight* (Accents Publishing, 2015).

"The biker girl" by Patricia Wellingham-Jones was previously published in *Moondance*, December 2006.

"Candy, Cigarettes, and Fairies" by Laura Madeline Wiseman was previously published in *Toad, The Journal & An Apparently Impossible Adventure* (BlazeVOX Books).

"To the Way I Walk" by Katy Yocom was previously published in *The Louisville Review*.

ABOUT THE EDITORS

Affrilachian Poet and Cave Canem Fellow, **Bianca Lynne Spriggs**, is a multidisciplinary artist from Lexington, Kentucky. Currently a doctoral candidate at the University of Kentucky, she holds degrees from Transylvania University and the University of Wisconsin-Milwaukee. Bianca is the recipient of a 2013 Al Smith Individual Artist Fellowship in Poetry, Artist Enrichment and Arts Meets Activism grants from the Kentucky Foundation for Women, and a Pushcart Prize Nominee. She is the author of *Kaffir Lily* (Wind Publications, 2010), *How Swallowtails Become Dragons* (Accents Publishing, 2011), and the forthcoming titles, *Call Her By Her Name* (Northwestern University Press, 2016) and *The Galaxy is a Dance Floor* (Argos Books, 2016). Bianca is the Literary Arts Liaison for the Carnegie Center for Literacy and Learning, creator and program director for The SwallowTale Project: Creative Writing for Incarcerated Women, as well as the Managing Editor for *pluck! The Journal of Affrilachian Art & Culture* and Poetry Editor for *Apex Magazine*.

Katerina Stoykova-Klemer is a bilingual author of several poetry books in English and Bulgarian, most recently *The Porcupine of Mind* (Broadstone Books, 2012, in English) and *How God Punishes* (ICU, 2014, in Bulgarian), which won the Ivan Nikolov National Poetry Prize. She is the editor of *The Season of Delicate Hunger: Anthology of Contemporary Bulgarian Poetry* (Accents Publishing, 2014), for which she also translated the works of 29 of the authors. She is the co-founder of the Poezia writing group, and for six years she hosted Accents—a radio show for literature, art and culture on WRFL in Lexington, Kentucky. In January 2010, Katerina launched the independent literary press Accents Publishing, which has published over 50 poetry books to date. Katerina co-wrote the award-winning independent feature film *Proud Citizen*, directed by Thom Southerland, and acted in the lead role. For her performance, she won a Special Jury Award for Acting at the 2014 Rivers Edge International Film Festival, and an Outstanding Acting Debut award at the 2015 Florida Film Festival.

CPSIA information can be obtained at www.ICGtesting.com
Printed in the USA
LVOW08s0411011215

464815LV00004B/4/P